# Sleeping like Spoons

# Sleeping like Spoons

## A MEMOIR

ED JONES

ISBN: 978-0-578-82795-7

All photographs, unless otherwise indicated, are courtesy of
the author.
Artist's painting by Deborah Boelter, page 168 and
back cover.

Cover and interior design: Ponderosa Pine Design

*To Mercedes Aguinaldo*

# Contents

# Preface

Throughout our twenty-one years together, Jose would periodically reach out and hold my arm and say, "Ed, you should write about us." This would typically be on a weekend at our breakfast table. Invariably I would laugh and say, "Jose, who in the world is going to be interested in a couple of ordinary gay guys living in New York?" And in many respects we *were* ordinary. But I knew he was saying this because he believed that, as a couple, we were not so ordinary. He really believed that our relationship had become a model for many people—straight and gay—and we (I) should try to put it in writing. I knew he was right.

Times have dramatically changed. Very few of us in the early 1980s could have anticipated that gay marriage would become the law of the land. And although we have a long way to go with employment and housing regulations and other discriminatory practices, the gradual acceptance of LGBTQ individuals in our society is encouraging.

That said, I present the following memoir as fulfillment of my obligation to my life partner to put our story in writing. It is simply an example of one gay couple during the 1980s and '90s in the United States with their shared joys, struggles, arguments, achievements, tragedies, and families. Despite our flaws as a couple, we endured.

So Jose, I have done what you asked of me. I wish I could have been more poetic, more descriptive, more eloquent, and perhaps even more brutally honest (although this writing is honest). But you were right. After all these years, I still hear from friends and family, "You were a model couple."

Finally, Jose, I dedicated this memoir to your mother. I was honored to sit by her side at her ninetieth-birthday celebration. I would have given anything if you could have been there too.

The two of us on my 50th birthday on Petit St. Vincent, 1997

## CHAPTER 1

# Passion and West Twenty-First Street

W e met on January 2, 1981, at a gay bar called Twilight on New York City's Upper East Side. A Japanese friend in Dallas, Aki, had introduced me to Twilight—popular among Asians—a year or so earlier during one of his visits to New York. I had frequented gay bars in Dallas during the late 1970s, but since moving to New York in fall 1979, I hadn't been going out much. A failed relationship in 1978 had left me reluctant to set myself up for another major disappointment. This explains why my roommate, Susan, was so surprised when I announced that I was going out. She and her visiting friend teased me about where I was going and what I should wear. I was evasive; I amused them; then I left.

The Twilight was small and dark, but friendlier than most gay bars where guys are eager to meet another but often put on an expression that sends the opposite signal. The game was to *act* uninterested. I know it doesn't make sense but a lot of it has to do with insecurity.

Inside, I got a drink and looked around. I don't remember talking to or dancing with anyone else, but I definitely noticed a very cute Asian guy who seemed approachable. He was about five foot seven and thin. His hair was thick, wavy, and slightly long. But what I remember most was the broad smile on his face. He seemed to be by himself. Although I was shy by nature, I approached him, asked his name, chatted for a while, and then asked him to dance. And so we did—on a very small, crowded dance floor.

**Jose, early 80s**

Finally, at a late hour and after several dances, he offered to drop me off at my apartment. His roommate, who it turns out was also at the bar, had a car and didn't seem to mind. During the drive home, we exchanged phone numbers, hugged, and said we'd be in touch. Gay guys know that this promise often results in nothing, so I didn't really count on a phone call. But I did expect to give him a call one day.

But the very next day, the phone rang. My friend Roy, visiting from Washington, DC, answered and then handed me the phone. "It sounds like . . . *Chewey?*"

I had no idea what he meant and took the receiver. On the line, a sweet, timid voice said, "This is Joey." I immediately recognized his voice and felt excited, surprised, and flattered that he had called me so soon. Emboldened, I invited him over that afternoon.

By the time he arrived, all other visitors, roommates, and friends were gone. We had the apartment to ourselves. I offered him a drink. He requested only a glass of water, so I abstained. (Joey, as I later learned, wasn't a drinker.) There was good chemistry and obviously a mutual attraction, given the long, exuberant conversation.

He told me about his background in the Philippines and his recent immigration to the States. He was an unemployed physician, having earned his MD degree in Manila, and was looking for a staff job at a hospital in New York, the city of his dreams. A few months earlier, he had made a false start in a urology internship on Staten Island. I talked about my immigration from Texas to New York. I was managing education programs at a nascent contemporary art museum, the New

Museum, in Greenwich Village.

As it turned night, there was excitement and energy in the air, with a spark just beneath the surface.

We went to my tiny bedroom, where I had built a sleeping loft to have enough room for a desk and clothing rack underneath. Halfway up the loft's ladder in the darkened room, Joey said, "I have a false leg."

I asked him to repeat himself, because at the time he had an accent I wasn't accustomed to. When I understood, I said, "It doesn't matter."

We made love four times that first evening.

That night would become the first of thousands of times I watched him carefully take off and later put on his special socks and then his leg. It was the beginning of many things, including my admiration, respect, and awe for the way he dealt with his handicap. Joey had lost a leg during medical school in Manila. It was an automobile accident. He was a pedestrian. I've since been told by his brothers and sisters that in Joey's typical fashion, he was joking even in his hospital bed after the amputation. According to his family, he said, "Well, I guess I won't be dancing anymore." Actually, nothing was farther from the truth. He danced whenever the mood struck him—at parties, on vacations, or just spontaneously.

Over the next days and weeks, we called each other frequently, and Joey would drop by almost every day, as he lived just a few blocks away. I was overjoyed.

Within a few weeks, Joey moved in and stayed for twenty-one years.

I have to believe it was fate. Two guys from opposite sides of the globe meeting by chance when they weren't expecting or looking for a partner. Meanwhile, it is important to remember that during early 1981, AIDS was barely beginning to present itself into the consciousness of the gay world, much less the general population. The disco era, saturated in free sex, was going strong with some parallel emerging activities by gay rights activists. The thought of gay men using condoms would have been considered a joke. Sure, you might be preventing some sort of venereal disease, but not to worry—whatever it was, it was curable with a dose of penicillin.

Very early on, I started to call him Jose rather than Joey, primarily because I instinctively wanted a pet name for him. No one else was calling him Jose. But it so happened that his given name would be more acceptable professionally in the long run. So over time, his "new" friends called him Jose, and his "old" friends called him Joey. To this day, I adjust my reference to him according to when he came to know people. To complicate the situation, his family, like all Filipino families, had special nicknames for him. His immediate family called him "Pet," which was short for "Pepito." That was the Filipino way.

In any case, Jose was with me and I was elated. I was almost thirty-three years old. The general perception was that gay guys don't stay together for any significant period of time, especially in those days. But I have to say, my family history and religious background always told me that you meet, love, and commit to a life partner. I attribute this mind-set to my parents, grandparents, and most of my older generation friends. Simply put, all of my role models stayed together. And it was clear that Jose had the same heritage—a conservative upbringing and solid parents.

Like most new couples, our early days together were first and foremost passionate. But cultural differences were problems. English was Jose's first language in school, but second at home. As I'd later learn, language wasn't his only problem when it came to communication. I believe he continued to think in Tagalog even when he spoke in English. Or another way of putting it, Jose wasn't verbally oriented. He would describe himself as verbally dyslexic. But in a sense, his verbal communication was extraordinary, especially as it uniquely combined with his body language and overall aura. However, little misinterpretations could lead to bigger misunderstandings. For example, he might cut himself off if he didn't know how to express himself at the moment. I would be left wondering what he was thinking.

These occasional problems were compounded by his job uncertainty at the time. During 1981, Jose was undecided about his medical specialization, so he searched for temporary staff positions at local hospitals. I helped him with his résumé and cover letters, and he was successful at pinning down decent jobs at hospitals in Queens and Brooklyn. One of them was Long Island College Hospital, which was at the foot of Brooklyn Heights, an attractive neighborhood accessible to Manhattan, where we lived.

One night, Jose asked me to come over and stay with him at the hospital during one of his rotations. I readily agreed, but it involved sleeping in residents' quarters, which equated to a college dormitory room. There were no double beds, so we slept together on the floor between the beds. In the middle of the night, someone opened the door and saw us lying there together in the dark. Whoever the person was, he didn't say anything but, "Oh, I'm sorry." We just laughed and went back to sleep.

We had a revolutionary experience the next year when Jose began his first year as a resident pediatrician at the New Jersey College of Medicine in Newark. He had decided that pediatrics was the field that appealed to him. And it suited him perfectly. He was the most natural-born pediatrician.

For the hospital's annual formal holiday party, Jose invited me to be his official guest. We were the only couple both dressed in tuxedos. It was the early 1980s! Gay couples were not a common sight in a traditional setting. In retrospect, his invitation represented a huge commitment on his part,

One of Jose's clinics or hospitals

as he was very focused on advancing his career and behaving in keeping with conventional American customs. This overt act might have caused his superiors to think twice about his advancement at the hospital.

Throughout his residency, Jose not only had to cope with the usual inhuman schedule that all residents have to deal with, but he also did it on one leg. When we first met, his false leg was so heavy he had to rest after two blocks of walking. But he never complained. He would just stop, wait, then go on. At the hospital, he kept going. And when he got home, after the regular drive through the Holland Tunnel from New Jersey to Manhattan, he would walk in the front door in his green hospital uniform and crash. A few hours later, he would get up and do it all over again.

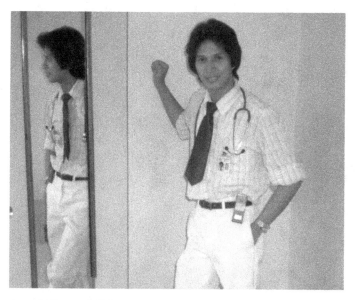

Jose, M.D., early 80s

During this time, Jose would stay in the residents' routine thirty-six-hour shift, then twelve hours off, then another long shift. I too was busy, at the museum, but not nearly as busy as he was. It was hard work, but we were excited about the unlimited prospects New York had to offer in the years to come. And in the meantime, we thoroughly enjoyed whatever time we had between our schedules in our modest apartment and on our modest budget. We could explore the city and easily find parking with Jose's handicap license plates. Occasionally we would find time to dine out inexpensively in Chelsea or Greenwich Village.

I had long since included Jose in formal and informal events at the museum. But that was an easy thing to do politically, as the New Museum was one of the more liberal institutions in the country. Regardless, it was exciting for us both when he showed up on opening nights when I would be bartending. The galleries were always packed. Sometimes I gave away drinks to artists, although I shouldn't have. Jose was totally mystified by the art (and admittedly so was I as a graduate intern). Much of my excitement had to do with just working at such a cutting-edge art venue in the Village, having just studied contemporary art as a graduate student at North Texas State University, where there was no significant contemporary art in sight.

I was earning next to nothing, and Jose was making little more than nothing as a resident. My days were long; his days were far longer. Sometimes, though, he would find energy from nowhere. Jose was like a playful little boy. He always maintained an extraordinary balance between a dedicated

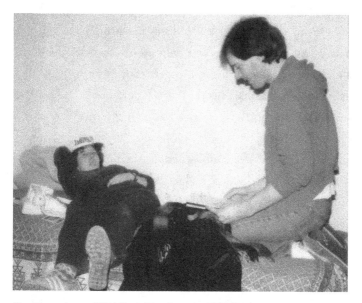

**Susan and me, 210 West 21st Street, 1981/82**

professional pediatrician on the one hand and a childlike, playful person on the other. Perhaps that's one reason little kids, especially his patients, were so at ease with him. He seemed like one of them.

We stayed in our Chelsea neighborhood apartment on West Twenty-First Street for about a year. It was a magical time.

Early on, my roommate Susan mentioned to me that suddenly we had a third person living with us. She wasn't exactly complaining, just expressing her thoughts, especially with regard to a New Yorker's sense of space. In New York, more than elsewhere, space is a significant consideration; it makes a difference in day-to-day situations. I understood and sympathized with her feelings. Susan was an artist who looked a little like a cartoon character. Short with curly brown hair and a far-off look in her eyes, she resembled a miniature Harpo Marx. That look was deceptive. She was very bright and absorbed everything going on, but often didn't say much about it. When she raised the question about Jose, I said, "I understand what you're saying. I didn't expect it to happen, but I'm glad it did."

After that, the three of us had a good rapport in the house. I compensated her for Jose's part of the rent, which was an important thing to do. Meanwhile, Jose naturally was absent most of the time because of his schedule. But more important, the two of them came to get along like two puppies. They would start teasing each other like six-year-olds. Before too long, they would be wrestling on the floor, roughly equivalent in size, and laughing out of control. I felt like the father

Jose and Susan, my two kids

of two kids, but I loved it. I would show mock disgust with their silliness, but they knew I was having just as much fun as they were.

Adjusting to each other, to New York, and to one another's cultures all at the same time were both difficult and exciting. Jose clearly had yearned to move to the great city for a long time, and so had I. Language continued to be somewhat of a problem throughout our relationship. But I realized years later that in his case it wasn't so much a problem with grammar as it was his spaced-out nature, which he clearly inherited from his mother. That nature was often frustrating but nevertheless part of his charm. Throughout his life people would react to Jose with a combination of befuddlement and humor, because he always got his words out in a unique way. And always with humor. Typically he would smile or laugh as he spoke, even when he wanted to make a serious point.

Our "super" (a New York standard term for the manager of the mechanics of the building) on West Twenty-First Street was somewhat quirky. He seemed to be in his midsixties and somewhat intellectual—not your typical super. His name was Mr. Davis. Somehow, spontaneously, when something suspicious happened in our apartment, we would say, "Mr. Davis did it." It was our way of saying, "I didn't do it" and blaming it on someone else. This convenient excuse lasted way beyond that year at 210 West Twenty-First Street. Even twenty years later, if suddenly a whole package of cookies "disappeared," one of us would swear, "Mr. Davis did it!" If I had been particularly flagrant about sneaking something, I would say, "Mr. Davis came over today, and he had a gun." This would make

Jose laugh. He was quick to laugh, always. And if I made a joke when he was drinking, he would burst out laughing, spewing whatever he was drinking all over himself.

## CHAPTER 2

# Two Families, Two Opposites

Jose and I moved to New York City for similar reasons. We both dreamed about the excitement and possibilities that New York had to offer. Ultimately, we fulfilled many of those dreams. As the years went by, we were able to mesh our ambitions and our support for one another, though occasionally our aspirations diverged. In the Filipino culture, they generally don't take things as seriously as Americans do. The United States had a dominant role there for decades, and in general many Filipinos emulated Americans. I often complained to Jose that he was giving too much emphasis to assimilating, while leaving behind a culture that had many positive attributes that the United States lacked. I would say to him, "Do what you want to do, but don't forget your heritage. Your culture has many things to offer that the American culture has left behind."

In the early years, I don't think he paid much attention to this. But years later, he began to gradually renew his appreciation for the culture he had left. He would talk more wistfully about the days in the Philippines—his great-uncle's orchard; the markets he would visit with his mother; going to the post office where his parents worked; and most of all, the family's apartment, where his classmates would stop by after school.

The apartment in metropolitan Manila was close to the University of Santo Tomas. His parents raised seven kids in that one-bedroom apartment (Val, Jose, Rosario, Tony, Lerida, Richard, and Tante). As often as Jose explained it, I never could quite picture it. His father had built a mezzanine where the five boys slept on mattresses according to seniority. Jose's two sisters had a place in the living room where they

**Family celebration at Chato's house**

slept, and the parents had the bedroom. Jose told me stories of complaining about too much noise and activity in the full apartment when he was trying to study for med school. On the other hand, I've also heard tales from his brothers and sisters about him keeping the lights on when everyone else was trying to sleep.

The family gave a high priority to education. But surprisingly, after completing undergraduate school, Jose's father discouraged him when he wanted to transfer from nursing school to med school. Jose always felt that his father was unnecessarily holding him back at that time.

Meanwhile, my upbringing was very conventional and mostly conservative as a boy growing up in the fifties and sixties in central Texas. This made it all the more amazing for

Jose's sister, Lery. Always laughter in that family

the two of us, from completely different cultures and regions of the world, to get together and stay together. I came from a small, conservative family with only one sibling, my sister, Fluffy. My sister and I were always like-minded. I always felt very supported by her. She was the more popular one, with lots of friends. I was the introverted, chubby kid who was terrible at sports.

My mother belonged to the National Society of the Colonial Dames of America, an organization of women who are lineal descendants of an ancestor who lived in one of the original colonies. She worked hard as a homemaker and was a devoted mother, wife, daughter to both parents, and community volunteer. My father was a jovial, gregarious guy who, after graduating from law school, enjoyed developing real estate properties in central Texas and dabbling in "Investments," as it said on his office door.

My maternal grandfather was an iconographic, fundamentalist preacher in our Presbyterian church. He was a larger-than-life figure who had married, baptized, counseled, preached to, and buried several local generations. He passed away in 1965, when I was a senior in high school, and left us with—I have to say—a somewhat guilty and judgmental heritage, which was the cause of me converting to the much more accepting Episcopal Church decades later.

Parallel to my conservative upbringing was Jose's traditional Filipino Catholic childhood. It's interesting to note that his family's background took a somewhat different direction in each of the seven siblings. But it is fair to say that Jose, among all of them, was most disenchanted with the

Church. We never discussed religious beliefs in great depth, but it was clear from his occasional statements that he wasn't interested in the institutional Catholic Church. Jose was very disillusioned with the Church's habit of taking money from relatively poor families while enriching itself and not necessarily putting the money to good use in the community. He was equally disgusted by the hypocritical habits of priests who often had mistresses or boyfriends. Jose was definitely not a prude, but he had no patience with hypocrisy. Meanwhile, he was spiritual in his own way.

If anything, *I* was more prudish. I always struggled with the polar pulls between my somewhat puritanical heritage and my newfound liberalism. And while my new direction brought me to New York to study and work in a contemporary

**Jose and me at an event**

art museum, my conservative background would sometimes emerge, which I would try to resist. Our relationship was happy and balanced, yet I am sometimes left feeling that my conservative core was a counterweight to Jose's infectiously joyful, free spirit. Friends and family have reassured me that it was just the way he wanted. Nevertheless, I'm left with some lingering guilt about my conservative nature and any dampening effect it might have had on him.

It helped a great deal to gradually get to know one another's family.

The first trip Jose and I made to California to meet his family the year after we met, was filled with both anxiety and anticipation on my part. Jose had a large, exuberant family, so unlike mine. His parents and siblings had all immigrated from Manila to Northern California in the late seventies except for his eldest brother, who was still in the Philippines. I wasn't sure how they would accept me as his partner. And I had very little experience with spending an extended amount of time in the midst of a big family.

My anxiety evaporated almost immediately. In those days, with gay couples, it was always a question of where you would sleep. Would the relationship be acknowledged like any other? When the time came, his mother, in her practical, straightforward way, said, "Here's where you'll stay." And she tossed two pillows onto a bed in one of the bedrooms. In other words, she couldn't be bothered by the details. This was a woman who raised seven children in inner-city Manila in a one-bedroom apartment while holding down a full-time job at the post office. Jose's brothers and sisters eventually figured out

Jose's mom with one of her 18 grandchildren. Jose had a strong resemblance to his mother in appearance and character

our relationship on their own, but from the beginning, they were totally welcoming to me.

One of Jose's sisters, Rosario (whom we call Chato), was very much like Jose in personality. You could say they were soul mates. Both were always full of laughter and animation, but very strong at the core. On one of our first trips to California, Chato had us up in a helicopter over San Francisco before we barely had landed at the airport. She loved to have fun. It was clear to me that Jose not only loved his sister very much, just as he loved all of his family, but he specifically identified with Chato. She couldn't have been friendlier to me.

I remember a phrase Chato used early on during our time together. Before she understood what our relationship was all about, I heard her refer to someone as "some sort of gay." The way she phrased it, the words sounded naive and innocent, somewhat quizzical. But it was without any disparagement whatsoever, just a natural observation.

Jose and Chato loved to have long talks on the phone, often early in the morning on weekends, but it could have been any time of the day. Always in Tagalog, the talks were sometimes bothersome to me because I had no idea what they were saying, except for the occasional sprinkling of English. Usually, the English words were monetary, as in "Blah, blah, blah four thousand dollars," "Blah, blah, blah six thousand dollars," and "Blah, blah, blah ten thousand dollars!" It left me wondering what the talk was all about. Early on, I would make suggestions, if asked, about money. Later I learned that this was not a good idea. The family had its own way of working things out. Nevertheless, Jose was very generous by nature. He often gave money to his family—especially to his parents. He would send them on trips or just mail cash.

It took me several years to get accustomed to joining his large family gatherings. Coming from a small family, and being somewhat of an introvert, I had a hard time. But as time went on, I started to love and admire the family. I called the little ones, ranging in age from zero to about seven or eight, "the swarming terrorists." They had great fun playing together, even when their ages were far apart. They looked after each other, with the usual occasional momentary squabbles, but always with a strong bond. Except for two of the girls and one of the boys who were born in the Philippines, all of the other fifteen nieces and nephews were born in the United

States after Jose and I met. During our second year together, they started coming in rapid order. Typically, Jose would be on the phone with his brothers and sisters, talking excitedly about the new family member. I was certainly happy for him and the family, but I had a hard time identifying with the excitement until later, when the younger kids were born. It took a while for me to bond with his siblings and to be part of the celebration. On average, though, during our twenty-one years together, one new niece or nephew would appear almost every year. And this steady family expansion gradually helped me integrate into the family myself. It was a wonderful feeling for someone who came from such a small, nongrowing family. And even better when the kids began to call me "Uncle Ed." That was very new to me, and completely heartwarming.

I've talked about Jose's family and their instant acceptance of us as a couple. It wasn't so simple with my family.

My parents took a while longer. Being very traditional and part of a well-established group of friends in our home-town, they needed more time to realize our situation. For several years, our visits to Texas would involve separate beds. Invariably we were presented as "roommates" to local Texan friends. That was the custom then, but it eventually changed. To their credit (at the time they were in their sixties), they welcomed Jose and took to him immediately, just as everyone did.

I think it was on Jose's first visit to Texas that I thought it would be a great idea to show him one of the few attractions in Waco that would be fun and relaxing for him. I suggested to my mother that she might call one of our friends who had a boat so that we could take an excursion on Lake Waco. That's exactly what we did, and that outing was the first of many that introduced local old friends to Jose. With his gregarious, outgoing nature, he easily fit in to just about any group or situation.

To fast forward now would be helpful. Simultaneous to my grandparents' heritage of conservatism, my parents were highly social, but grounded in their era, which involved attending college during the Depression. That said, remarkably twenty years after we met, Jose was seated at the front row of the church at my father's funeral. This was the same church where my grandfather had preached for thirty-five years and during that time wouldn't have given a thought to welcoming

Jose with my parents and my aunt Mary Frances in Waco, Texas

gay couples, black couples, or anyone else other than the usual WASPs. The church was packed for the funeral. After all, my father had spent eighty-seven years in the community. But to have this diminutive Asian guy seated third from my mother on such an occasion said much about the progress of his acceptance into the family, the openness of the historically conservative church, and the community in general.

CHAPTER 3

# Ambivalent Assimilating

We were constantly assimilating into one another's lives and families. That was a big component of our ongoing joy and sometimes frustration. Both the joy and frustration never ended, but clearly the joy tipped the balance.

During our early years, in the early eighties I needed to pay attention to my own assimilation into Jose's culture. I have to confess, even though I always reminded him to remember his culture and not leave it behind, part of me wanted him to assimilate sooner rather than later. Surprisingly, this ambivalence didn't make for any particular conflict between the two of us. It was more of a conflict within myself.

Grounded in my native country, I never had been faced with the need to immerse myself in another culture. Jose brought a chunk of his culture with him to the States—large numbers of family and friends. I playfully referred to his med school colleagues as "the Filipino mafia." Many of his classmates immigrated to the States as soon as they were able. And many of them chose New York as their destination, just as countless other immigrant groups had done for centuries. Meanwhile, most of his classmates were straight. Since we didn't make a practice of announcing our sexuality, it probably made for some confusion. But I must give his friends credit. They readily accepted me, and I suppose learned on their own over time what our relationship was all about. Actually, the same goes for my old friends. I just didn't believe in the need to "out" oneself, and certainly not anyone else.

I am very much aware that nowadays the younger generation would expect a more direct and open statement about one's sexual orientation. And I have great appreciation and admiration for all of the gay activists who helped make life easier for the rest of us. There are times when I wish I had been more of an activist. And I hold a certain amount of guilt. But we make our choices, and Jose and I basically chose the same path: don't cover it up, but don't force the issue onto someone who will accept us in their own time. After he passed away, I maintained strong friendships with Jose's colleagues at the hospital. I doubt if he ever made any specific announcement to them about our relationship. But in their own time, they accepted me because they loved him just as he was. And Jose was very easy to love.

Our two paths leading up to our meeting on January 2, 1981, were obviously different. My background was from upper-middle-class America. I was born with many advantages in terms of family resources, connections, and racial privilege. I shouldn't overstate this. My parents experienced the hardships of the Depression, and my grandparents struggled along with everyone else to hold everything together. Nevertheless, from the earliest age I can remember, I had no worries about living a comfortable life. Jose, on the other side of the globe in Manila, experienced hardships that he was not totally aware of at the time. Although they were crammed into very close quarters, the family always spoke of their home in a happy, jolly spirit. They fought over, and shared, favorite blue jeans that probably fit several of the brothers and sisters. But come time for dinner, they all knew that their father expected them to be together at the dinner table at six o'clock sharp, or someone would be in trouble.

Jose with his parents, nieces, and nephews

For the Aguinaldos, it was about teamwork and sharing. It took me years to understand that Jose's culture was about how the younger or less advantaged in the family would rely on help from their elders. For example, his well-off uncle paid for Jose's med school. But the help was by no means automatic. Jose had to approach his uncle and ask for help. Then it was forthcoming immediately. What I never understood in the long run, however, was that Jose didn't bother to maintain a connection with his uncle. They kept in touch through the general family network, but there was no special connection. Nowadays we would call it "paying it forward."

The flip side of this situation was Jose's famous generosity. He gave to everyone without expectation of reciprocation. One of my most vivid memories of his generosity had to do with his younger cousin, who moved to New York City in the early '90s. Known as a spoiled brat, John was starting his college education at NYU. Without hesitation, Jose immediately began to search for an apartment for his cousin—not an easy task in New York City under the best of circumstances. Jose managed to find a large (by New York standards), comfortable one-bedroom apartment in the Village, which was a highly desirable location. He also tossed in some furniture and guaranteed the lease. Later, when John moved to another, more upscale location in the Village and shared space with roommates, Jose guaranteed the lease again.

After about a year, Jose began to get calls from the landlord, who hadn't been paid due rent. Apparently John had moved out but overlooked the fact that Jose (as lease guarantor) was still liable for the remaining roommates who weren't paying the rent. Finally, after months of negotiations, the problem was settled. Throughout the ordeal, Jose rarely, if ever, complained. I was beginning to absorb the cultural difference. In the process, I gained tremendous respect for Jose's generosity, perseverance, focus, hard work, and lack of bitterness. It became increasingly clear that he was a person who continually looked forward, and simply ignored or failed to see negative experiences.

CHAPTER 4

# Chelsea to Brooklyn

Living in Manhattan's Chelsea neighborhood during 1981–1982, one of our indulgences was to walk down to the Village. There we would typically go to a Chinese restaurant, Big Wok, and stuff ourselves on less than ten dollars—for the two of us! Then we would slowly walk—due to Jose's heavy leg and our stuffed bellies—back to West Twenty-First Street. Once home, both of us would have to rest and go to sleep early. During those early years, I don't recall reading myself to sleep, as I did years later. Typically it would be sex that would bring on sleep.

At that time living and working in Manhattan's concrete jungle, I was anxious to get back to some green grass and trees. My friend Maureen at the New Museum mentioned some property in Virginia. Maureen was the person I interviewed with as a prospective intern when I first moved to New York. My adviser at City College told me to contact Ms. Stewart. It didn't take long for me to realize that I was older than Ms. Stewart, but after she hired me as an intern, we soon became friends. And as the earliest arrivers at the museum each morning, we got into the habit of gossiping and talking about any news of the day.

For some reason one day, Maureen showed me photographs of some lush property in Virginia and I decided to spend a week of vacation time at this place, simply attracted by the missed greenery. Jose unfortunately was obliged to continue with his program at New Jersey Medical, so I set off by myself with very little money.

I got to the location and found a campsite where I rented a space and slept in my rented car. To be honest it was a fairly ordinary green-dense property, but as a newcomer to New York and as a homesick Texan, I was taken with its trees.

After about a day and a half, I got a call from Jose. He told me he was lonely and wanted me to come home. That's all it took. I started back to New York right away, without hesitation. What more could I have wanted but to be missed? It was an easy decision to make. Jose wanted me home.

In those days, Chelsea was still very much in transition, but it soon became a hot gay neighborhood. And later still, it would become home to many high-end galleries a little farther to the west. Our apartment was on the ground floor, its front door directly ahead as you entered the building. Once inside our apartment, you looked down a long hallway. Like many other prewar apartments in New York, the bedrooms and bathroom were to one side of the hallway. In our case, our bedroom was immediately to your right. It was about the size of a closet.

Next was the one bathroom, then our roommate Susan's bedroom, which was the size of, well, a larger closet. Beyond that was a short hallway to the right leading to the kitchen (with an out-of-use dumbwaiter). And straight ahead at the end of the main hallway were the living and dining rooms, both small, but typical of early-twentieth-century design, with high ceilings.

Our tiny bedroom—with its exposed brick and (self-built) platform bed and ladder—was a wonderful cocoon. It was the place where our romance began and flourished. It was where Jose would rise early and commute to Newark to his first-year residency in pediatrics, and it was where I would also rise early and walk to the New Museum to unlock; turn on the lights; and, as the morning hours went by, greet the rest of the staff.

The loft bed was just high enough to walk beneath it and to accommodate a makeshift closet with a clothes rod. There was also enough space for a large desk, which we shared. Below the bed was a floor lamp that dimly lit the area when one of us would rise first.

One of my most vivid memories of that room—apart from being the epicenter of our romance—was early one morning when I was dressing for work and Jose was still in bed. This was atypical, since he would ordinarily rise first, or he would still be away at the hospital during a thirty-six-hour shift. On this particular morning, I was about to leave for work. The room was barely glowing from the lamp. Jose stretched out his hand from the bed above and said, "You are my inspiration." I was overwhelmed. It was clear to me that if either one of us was an inspiration for the other, it was Jose. I don't know why he said that, but it stunned me in the most exhilarating way and remained with me forever.

Other memories of that apartment include a few small but festive parties. Mostly it was the three of us (Jose, myself, and Susan) having ordinary, silly fun. For a while, we tried to scrape off the old paint and give the place more of an updated look. But the work of scraping so many layers of paint and the prospect of having to give up the lease after two years made it not worthwhile.

In the summer of 1982, we were forced to give up our two-year sublease. The only practical option at the time was to take advantage of Jose's residents' quarters at Brooklyn's Maimonides Hospital, where he had transferred to continue his pediatric training. It was a very conventional '60s building, but spacious in comparison to the squeezed spaces of Manhattan. We were offered a large one-bedroom apartment just across from the hospital in the mainly Hasidic Jewish neighborhood of Borough Park. As an Anglo/Asian gay couple in the midst of large Jewish families where the men wore long black coats, tall black hats, and sported long, curly sidelocks, we were most definitely in the minority. The Jewish women wore wigs in the custom of covering their heads in public. Abundant baby carriages made it difficult to navigate the sidewalks.

Nonetheless, the location convenience made a big difference on those many nights when Jose would call from across the street and say, "Put on the rice. I'll be home in thirty minutes." It didn't matter too much to Jose what the meal consisted of as long as we had rice. I learned early on how to use a rice cooker. He would arrive exhausted and hungry. Often he would have to go back to work afterward and complete a long shift.

For some reason the building staff hadn't cleaned the apartment when it was vacated. Coincidentally, one of Jose's friends from the Philippines, part of the "Filipino mafia," was just vacating. We spent a day or more cleaning the grease from the kitchen countertop and everywhere else. This was the result of Filipino traditional cooking, which involves significant amounts of fat and grease. Fortunately, Jose learned to adapt that tradition to American taste. And although in later years his mom told me that she had taught her son how to cook, Jose shared with me that it was his dad who taught him the art of Filipino cooking without a recipe.

We settled into the residents' quarters. It was very basic and spare, with linoleum, not wood, floors, but it felt spacious compared to our former West Twenty-First Street digs, where we had spent our first year together. Since we were so poor (and left our built-in loft behind), we put our mattress on the floor in the bedroom. The living room too was mostly bare, but that was fine with us. Jose had many friends in the building because they were also residents at the hospital and because he readily made friends.

This proved to be a good thing.

The very day of our move, just after driving solo over the Brooklyn Bridge with our belongings, as Jose was at work, I saw an old station wagon coming straight toward me in the middle of the street. I had nowhere to go. The driver, who

47

quite likely was drunk, smacked me head-on. I passed out momentarily and then looked around. People were gathering, wanting to help.

I realized that blood was dripping from my chin. I reached down where we kept a box of tissues and pulled out the entire box's contents and jammed it onto my lower lip. I kept it there until the ambulance brought me to the emergency room. When a nurse asked me to pull the tissue off, she said, "Do you want a plastic surgeon?" I nodded yes.

After an hour or so, the surgeon came, and within another half hour, Jose showed up with another resident friend. I felt strange having an audience at close range as the surgeon stitched my lip. But it was also very comforting to have a second and a third opinion close at hand. This remained the case for the next twenty years.

## CHAPTER 5

# *Being Supportive*

A relationship, apart from raising children for some couples, typically involves sex, sleeping like spoons next to one another, mutual financial and emotional support, sharing all of the highs and lows of life, and perhaps most important, that "exclusive network of two" that continues throughout the day when you're not physically together. This might involve a quick phone call about a funny thing you read in the paper, a friend's emergency, a complaint at work that you need to vent about, or ideas for a future shared vacation. Often Jose would call me at work early in the day to say, "Did you see the article in the paper about . . ." Well, usually I *hadn't*, since he was reading *The Wall Street Journal* and I was reading *The New York Times*.

It is impossible to define what makes a successful couple. To look at us, it was an unlikely match—a short, caramel-skinned, very young-looking Asian guy with a tall, light-skinned, very traditional-looking Anglo guy. But it was

**Jose, Ellen, and me, 40ᵗʰ birthday party at Ellen's apartment in Greenwich Village**

clear to us fairly early in our relationship that many other people, straight and gay, observed us and saw a genuine bond. We were conscious of not being physical around others. It was a different era. But it was clear that we were a team. We respected each other; we consulted each other; we listened to each other; we admired each other; we helped each other—all with great pleasure and pride, and without pretense. Jose provided that miraculous spontaneity; I was more measured yet tuned into the times. The combination formed a refreshing match. When we showed up at any number of events over the years, we were seen as a unique, authentic couple.

Despite his quirky way with language, Jose had a way of expressing himself almost poetically. Over the years he would say, "Oh Ed, are we always going to be like this?" Meaning, we are so great together, will this continue indefinitely?

I would always say, "Yes, Jose. Always, always, always."

Then he would say, "Another fifty years?"

I'd laugh and say, "Jose, that makes me ninety-eight years old and you would be ninety-four."

Then he would talk about how healthy we were, how both of our families had strong genes, and how we took good care of each other. The years did not matter. It was his way of affirming our lifelong commitment and joy of our partnership.

Romance came out on special occasions such as birthdays, or just spontaneously. Several times he came home with tickets to a great destination with no particular occasion in mind. He just wanted to enjoy life. He took great pleasure in giving, whether it was gifts to me or to his family or friends.

Jose's sister, Chato, was and is frequent host for family gatherings in Union City, CA

The last New Year's Eve we spent together was typical. We had no plans. Ordinarily, the lack of plans would bother me much more than it would bother him. I have a hard time not celebrating major holidays, while Jose would be just as happy to go home, take off his leg, and watch TV. But on December 31, 2001, I called Jose from work and told him I had read about a concert at the Cathedral of St. John the Divine. This is a grand cathedral near our then Morningside Heights apartment, where I attended services fairly regularly and where many special performances were presented. On this occasion, Judy Collins was scheduled to sing, along with other performers of all sorts. I was a little surprised that Jose agreed without hesitation to meet me there.

By 9:00 p.m., roughly two thousand people had followed the same idea. The cathedral was so crowded that we had to huddle in one of the alcoves far away from the performers. We sat on some cold marble steps, stayed long enough to hear a few songs, and then drove down the street to one of our favorite neighborhood restaurants, Henry's. It was a cozy, friendly place yet large enough not to worry so much about a reservation. It too was full of people celebrating in their own way. After a nice dinner, we headed home just before midnight. Walking into the apartment, I assumed we would go to bed right away. But inside the living room I found a wonderful surprise. Jose had stopped at the apartment on his way to the cathedral and decorated our table with New Year's Eve decorations, champagne, and chocolate truffles (his favorite food). We had been together for twenty-one years, and this is what he did to please me.

"Enjoy life to the fullest" was Jose's motto. But equally he believed in hard work and its ability to bring opportunities to you. Much of his enjoyment was directly connected to his generosity and daily unselfish acts.

As already highlighted, Jose was well known for his generosity—with his spirit and with tangibles. He took great pleasure from giving to others. Many times he came home with gifts— everything from gourmet chocolates to tickets to the Caribbean, which he did more than once. Sometimes he would bring little gifts to me that he had randomly run across in antiques shops. It was very touching. On more than one occasion, he brought antique pocket watches and gold chains. It made an impression on me for several reasons. He was always thinking of me when he was just browsing

Jose on one of our excursions

through shops of all sorts. And he loved to shop, preferably at Bergdorf's! But it also meant that he had some image of me wearing a pocket watch, perhaps in a vest. What a sweet gesture! I never wore them, but I was so excited just to receive them. He was quite old-fashioned but contemporary at the same time; sentimental, but anxious to keep up with trends.

Jose's generous spirit manifested itself throughout his life—from the small incidental daily occurrences to major acts of kindness. He was probably the only person in New York City who would go out of his way to give a parking space to someone. If he was about to leave a coveted space and he saw someone searching for a spot, he would approach them and signal that he was leaving. Sometimes they weren't even looking for a spot; he just wanted to be sure that they knew he was vacating one just in case.

Despite the generosity of tangibles and parking spots, his generosity of spirit was even greater: with the families of his patients who he would go out of his way to spend time with; with his nieces and nephews he would talk to endlessly about the importance of education; and with me, with whom he was hugely patient (up to a point).

I suppose the greatest evidence of Jose's generosity is the joy he got from the little and the big efforts he put into it. As always, his response would be a big smile and often a big laugh. Jose carried laughter with him every day. He had several varieties ready to come out spontaneously. His giggle came out most often, in response to something that struck him as amusing at the office, at home, in a restaurant, anyplace, anytime. Then he had a very loud "Ha!," which he

Jose picking fruit looking like a poster boy for some apple juice brand in Catskill, NY

would combine with other laughs. I think he picked up the "Ha!" from our roommate during our first year together, as Susan had a similar expression. But his best laugh was authentic, full-blown, and out of control. It was always ready in any unpredictable situation. And it was contagious. And although people around him, including often myself, frequently didn't fully understand what he was laughing about, that made it all the more amusing.

He had a little boy countenance with teasing big eyes and fingers ready to tickle, counterbalanced by the wise sensibility of an empathetic physician who had experienced great personal challenges and trauma. He was a contemporary Pied Piper to his hundreds of enthusiastic little patients. When you roll all that up into a sparky little man with beautiful caramel skin, a boyish face, and a bow tie, it formed a disarmingly innocent and endearing presence, but with an inner core of steel.

Once when we had a minor disagreement and I appeared offended, he apologized, saying that his profession had caused him to desensitize and distance himself from some human emotional situations. This helped me understand his reactions to innumerable similar situations after that.

Jose constantly reminded me (by example) how to be youthful and not take life too seriously. He looked for that spark in others—friends, family, even strangers—and lit it up. It came naturally to him. Hundreds of times I watched him work that magic, which he wasn't even aware of.

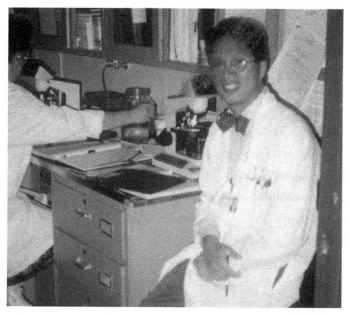

Jose at one of his many clinics. He usually worked two jobs.

For instance, when we lived on West 100th Street from 1993 to 2002, we would take the elevator to the ground floor early in the morning on our way to work. At this time of day, most people want to speak as little as possible. But Jose would greet the doorman, Mr. Long, with a big smile and say, "So, are you going fishing today?" (This would be in midwinter.) The doorman would chuckle. Like everyone else, he wasn't sure how to react. It was a joke, right? But the absurdity of the question still had a piece of honesty to it that called for an answer. Mr. Long would smile and say, "No, it's too cold today." Jose might then add, "You better go catch that one everybody else wants to catch!" Then, as we walked away, just as I observed in countless similar situations, the doorman would be smiling, but with a curious expression of delight and confusion. It was an exquisite moment that repeated itself again and again.

In the mid eighties, Jose was excited about an opportunity to occupy his own office in a group practice in Spanish Harlem on First Avenue. It was a beehive of small rooms. At least two other doctors were practicing there and serving the dense population of Hispanics in a neighborhood long established with all of its traditions, shops, churches, community services, and rich cultural activities.

When Jose got his assigned room in the group, I helped him with the challenging job of cleaning it. It came with a standard examination table and just a few basic accessories. But it was the focal point for a new start for Jose in the profession that he had worked so hard for, including years of grueling studies, internships, and residencies.

The examination room was dirty, but we cleaned and cleaned, doing it gladly with the thought that this would be the place for launching his career in pediatrics. Finally, it was done. It was ready for patients. We put up clinical signs on the wall along with colorful pictures and objects that would present a welcoming place for toddlers.

The first day arrived. I suppose I was busy at the museum. Then the evening came, and Jose arrived back home. He had not treated one single patient. I felt so bad for him, but I managed to be encouraging. And in his determined way, he managed to express optimism. Nevertheless, it was a very sad evening. Both of us struggled not to let the obvious disappointment of the moment overtake us.

However, before long, the patients, families, and friends began to show up. I'm sure word of mouth worked, given Jose's personality and his child-friendly and parent-friendly manner. Soon he was plenty busy as he built the trust of the families in the community, and kids began to ask for him.

The difficult challenges strengthened our relationship over the years as we helped each other get through tough times. We enjoyed being supportive of one another. Both of us had parents who modeled such behavior for decades. In their own ways, they had worked out a partnership that was not easy, but worth the effort and ultimately very rewarding. That's not to say that there weren't bumps along the way. There were.

But I think we both learned from our experiences with each other and from our parents that some things work as a couple:

Be a good listener.

Pay attention to your partner even when you've had a long day and you're tired. It doesn't take so much effort simply to listen and to demonstrate that you're listening.

And be supportive. Agree with him! Unless it would be harmful to do otherwise.

One example: On occasion when I would whine incessantly about anyone who might be causing me grief, Jose would listen and say, "I'm going to take out a contract on [that person]." That's all I needed to hear. He was paying attention, he was taking my side, and he was interjecting a little humor, which always helps.

CHAPTER 6

# The Eighties in New York

N ew York City was an exciting but dangerous place in the early '80s. The city was struggling to come out of its financial crisis. Drugs and their connected crime problems permeated the fabric of the city. The subways were run-down and covered in graffiti. People looked over their shoulder everywhere they went. Nevertheless, there was an undercurrent of optimism.

A new president had just been elected, and regardless of your political persuasion, you felt a sense of imminent change. And that sense energized discussions about shifting public policy. The early years of the Reagan administration paralleled the early years of the AIDS epidemic. It became increasingly frustrating as time went on that the new president would not make direct mention of the horrible epidemic that killed thousands of people in the United States during his first term alone. Moving plays, books, and personal stories were filling the theaters, bookstores, and newspapers—including horrific stories about lifelong partners being put in body bags by funeral homes to avoid contact with AIDS victims. It was a frightening time—especially to be gay. On a nearly daily basis, the obituary section of *The New York Times* featured haunting photographs of once-vibrant young men, many of whom were the most creative among us: choreographers, designers, composers, performers of all types. Inevitably, the gay scene—the clubs, Christopher Street, Fire Island—was devastated and filled with a sense of sadness, frustration, despair, anger, and rage. It was nightmarish and it was heartbreaking.

The first time I recognized AIDS in a friend face-to-face was in about 1983. Jose, Susan, and I were meeting for dinner in our old Chelsea neighborhood. We happened to run into a young guy who lived in our building. After a brief chat on the sidewalk, we walked away. I was stunned that this vigorous, attractive young man was showing signs of the horrible virus that was creeping into our population at an accelerating rate. Surprisingly, Jose and Susan didn't seem to recognize its effects right away.

During those years, I was focused on building a new education department at the New Museum. If it wasn't at the epicenter of the contemporary art world at the time, the New Museum was close to it, largely due to the extraordinary energy, vision, and wisdom of Marcia Tucker, its founding director.

Most of the staff's desks were in a single small room in

a corner of the New School building on Fifth Avenue and Fourteenth Street. Even though I was a lowly intern, Marcia would share her desk with me and we'd push the telephone back and forth depending on who an incoming call was for. With tremendous encouragement, she gave me total latitude regarding the education programs. And as time went on, she gave me far more credit than I deserved for the accomplishments of this new department. She was immeasurably important in my transition from grad student to professional in New York's museum/visual arts/nonprofit community.

It was an exhilarating time at the museum. We didn't really have to have staff meetings. The office was so small that we could overhear every conversation, whether it was a curatorial planning meeting, a chat with a board member, a fight with a boyfriend, or some serious gossip. Staff was always immediately, completely informed.

Each new exhibition brought renewed excitement and great anticipation by the art-loving public. After pressing their noses against the glass front doors before the opening, hundreds of members and friends would flood the lobby of the New School and the single small gallery, where challenging and provocative works of art awaited them. I would man one of the bars in the lobby, greet friends, and give away far too many free drinks. Invariably, Jose would show up, often with friends in tow.

Occasionally he would drop by the office to pick me up and chat with colleagues. Simple occasions like that were remarkable to me. Just a few short years before, I could only have dreamed of sharing my partner openly with colleagues who welcomed him with genuine affection. The openness was liberating yet sometimes difficult to absorb for someone who had recently left a closeted life in Texas. It *was* 1981—a very different era.

We were benefiting from the slow, hard-won, incremental freedoms and recognition for gays. To this day, I regret that I didn't play an active role in that liberation. I give enormous credit to those who courageously fought for gay rights while we were devoting all of our energies to career and to each other. We weren't indifferent to the hard-won progress; we just gave our energy to other things. We lived as a couple first and foremost, and secondly as gay, or biracial, or international, or multicultural. We didn't try to hide anything, but at the same time we didn't put it in your face. This was most apparent with our families.

At about this time Marcia discussed some new concerns at a staff meeting. She explained that during a recent meeting with a colleague from another "alternative space," she was made aware that the New Museum wasn't as inclusive as it should have been regarding artists of color. Marcia acknowledged this and asked us for ideas. She, or someone else in the room, suggested that we start with open dialogue. And then she asked for volunteers. My right hand began to rise—perhaps a combination of naïveté and helium. In any case, with plenty of help I organized a "Minority Artist Dialog Series" over the next few years. Venues included Marcia's apartment, my apartment, and the museum itself. The programs ranged from highly charged venting sessions to constructive exchanges that led to new collaborations and evolving programs within the organization.

I would like to think that I helped to bring a broader scope to the New Museum's many programs, but I was reminded by many of the artists who participated in the dialog series that they had been involved in similar efforts in the past and that one step forward was often followed by one or two steps backward. Hopefully that would not prove to be the case in this instance. Regardless of its effects in the long run, I greatly benefited from the wisdom and rich experience of numerous artists of all colors during that period.

Jose knew absolutely nothing about contemporary art. In all innocence he would ask, "Ed, is that a art?"

"Yes, it is art," I would reply.

Jose was completely open-minded and exhilarated by the openings at the New Museum—as was I. Marcia came to know Joey as she embraced the museum's extended family.

The last time the three of us were together (Jose, Marcia, and myself) was at the opening of her last show at the New Museum. It was at the larger facility, in SoHo—far larger than the venue in the old days in the Village at the New School (but far smaller than its current structure on the Bowery). She hadn't seen us in a few years. In the midst of a large "downtown" art crowd, she spotted Jose and offered a big hug, saying, "Joey, Joey, Joey!" For me, it was a wonderful moment. That evening, which was full of excitement and reflection for me, encapsulated more than a decade of my life in New York.

I stumbled through this period with plenty of naïveté, including applying to the internship program at the National Endowment for the Arts' Office of Minority Concerns. (This was just prior to meeting Jose.) Much to my surprise, I was accepted into the program. On the same day, I received notice from the NEA that my application for a grant toward my education outreach program had been accepted. I was ecstatic. Thanks to the NEA, many doors were opening for me, all at the same time. And fortunately, I was able to move to Washington, DC, start to work at the Office of Minority Concerns, and defer the grant for my new education program until after I returned to New York.

On day one at the NEA, the other interns, or fellows, were greeted by their respective sponsoring programs. When I walked into the Office of Minority Concerns and met the director and other program staff, it was quickly apparent that they had expected this Ed Jones to be of a different color. It hadn't occurred to me until that moment that their expectations had been that their intern would be African-American. No one specifically mentioned it, but it was apparent despite their genuinely warm and welcoming reception. Nevertheless, in the moment it was a surprise—both a little humorous and a little sad, since the assumption was that white people wouldn't be interested in that office. But as time went by during that fall internship, we worked well together.

I'd like to think that I made a significant contribution to the program. And by the end of my internship, the director offered me a permanent job. I was very grateful and gratified that I had justified myself to her, but as tempting as the offer was, I decided to return to New York and the New Museum, where I had a grant waiting for me to officially start a new education component at the vibrant, rapidly growing organization. It was an opportunity I excitedly returned to at the end of 1980, never expecting to meet a young, attractive Filipino doctor at a gay bar on the Upper East Side of Manhattan just a few weeks later.

## CHAPTER 7

# My Career Develops

Only a decade earlier, I was an assistant bank examiner at the Federal Reserve Bank in Dallas, surrounded by all guys in suits. Like my peers, I was involved in the usual postcollege activities of the '70s: building a new career, dating girls, socializing, drinking, and exploring. But unlike most of my peers, I was doing all of this out of mere momentum and expectation. It didn't take long for me to understand that I didn't want to stay on this path—not that I had a clear alternative plan for the future. It just didn't feel right.

I quit my job at the Fed after just a year or two and entered an MBA program at the University of Texas at Arlington. This move allowed me to move away from a nine-to-five routine but still maintain the possibility of continuing in a general career in the world of business or banking. I was allowing myself to experiment. But soon it became clear to me that this too was not the world I wanted to live in. I finished the degree, but began to explore all sorts of alternatives.

Meanwhile, I needed to pay the rent.

I got a job as a waiter at one of the many local steak restaurants in Dallas, much to the shock of my parents. "Why would our son, who just completed an MBA degree, suddenly decide to wait tables?" I couldn't satisfy their expectations, but the job allowed me the flexibility to think . . . and to play. But I was closing in on thirty and mindful that this was only a temporary situation. What sort of career would motivate me? How did I *really* want to spend the next decade, or two, or three?

I returned to graduate school, but this time in art history at North Texas State in Denton. After commuting from Dallas during the first semester, I rented a tiny apartment next to the campus. This was part of my years-long downward mobile path. But it felt good and liberating to be studying something that truly engaged me. I got excited to think it was a field where I could actually pursue a career. In fact, it felt good enough to then accelerate. After completing most of my course work, I was determined to move to New York, the center of the art world. And so I transferred to City College, New York, to complete the degree and seek employment.

During my years at the New Museum, I gained a solid grounding in the nonprofit sector. And by working in a particularly small organization, I had an opportunity to be exposed to all aspects of that field—program design and implementation, staffing, board relations, fund-raising, external relations. I thrived in an environment where the museum was gradually establishing itself as a unique entity between the traditional museum world with a professional curatorial staff and exhibition schedule on the one hand, and the rapidly growing field of artist-run organizations on the other.

Much to the distress of my graduate adviser, who wanted me to pursue a more traditional museum track, I was drawn to the idiosyncratic world of artist spaces. New York was the epicenter of that growing national movement, which consisted of well over a hundred nonprofit galleries founded and run by passionate, professional individuals who shared a vision of organizations that would first and foremost serve living artists (who, for the most part, were not gaining deserved attention from commercial galleries or established museums or the general public).

At one point in the early '80s I served on the board of the National Association of Artists Organizations. All members of NAAO were committed to maintaining their noninstitutional structure and character. But as the number of the organizational members grew, their sheer size and scale pulled them toward a more traditional board, staff, and program design. Many chose to maintain their small-scale operations with the intention of sustaining close relationships with the community of artists they served. Meanwhile, NAAO had a strong relationship with the National Endowment for the Arts, which bolstered our involvement with the field across the country.

I was still on the learning curve regarding the recent history of the many nascent and thriving artists' organizations whose missions and focus were tied to the local and regional

**Introducing a panel of curators and artists at the New Museum, early 80s.**

needs of artists. It was inspiring for me to get acquainted with the prime movers and visionaries who had established the various groups. And although collectively it was a very nontraditional spectrum of organizations, I hope that I occasionally brought a worthwhile perspective to the table with my atypical background.

Time passed. After five years at the New Museum, during which I continued and expanded the lecture series around current issues in contemporary art, organized outreach programs for students in public schools, trained docents, and managed volunteers and interns, I took a sabbatical to complete my graduate degree in art history/museum training.

I returned to the New Museum briefly, but decided to cross over to the philanthropic side. In other words, I joined the sector that provided support to the field where I had been working and learning for the previous five years.

Naïvely, I thought that it would be a relatively easy transition. Little did I know that the field of arts philanthropy is extremely finite and very challenging to enter. After numerous attempts and what seemed to be an endless number of months, I was offered a position as grants officer at the Metropolitan Life Foundation. I was thrilled, but I had no idea how wrenching it would be to adjust to one of the most traditional and conservative corporations in the country, having spent the previous five years in a rather radical arts environment. But despite the corporate context of my new job, I was motivated by the ongoing interaction with some of the most creative individuals in the country who were professionals in the performing and visual arts world. And it was a new world for me, as I had little knowledge of the performing arts landscape at the time.

In the new office I had to learn to deal with the hierarchy and bureaucracy of a large multinational corporation. Out in the field, I was learning the ins and outs of a vast array of organizations in the arts world with all of their incredible programs in dance, theater, music, and the visual arts. It *was* a challenge, but I never lost sight of the fact that it was also a privilege. And it was humbling to review the burgeoning flow of proposals from arts organizations of all types and sizes, while keeping an eye on a relatively modest arts budget within the Metropolitan Life Foundation itself.

During that time I got acquainted with a very collegial group of arts funders in New York—Grantmakers in the Arts/NYC—and simultaneously with Grantmakers in the Arts/USA. Very quickly I learned that this network was a valuable resource, especially for a newcomer such as myself. We relied on one another to supplement our knowledge and understanding of the groups that were applying to us for funding, although each one of us had our own particular set of guidelines and constraints.

An additional perk was that Jose and I enjoyed attending performances regularly as part of my effort to get acquainted with the field I was responsible for directing money toward. In the process, Jose became quite a dance critic, often using descriptors that were just a little off, or *way* off, in his postperformance summaries. Typically these discussions were over a late dinner in a quiet restaurant where we could unwind after a long day involving numerous patients for him and copious incoming grant proposals for me. It was an exciting time for both of us and continued to be as long as we were together. Over the years, Jose came to know many of my colleagues in the funding world as well as many of the performing and visual artists involved in the organizations I was supporting.

Little did I know what was around the corner. But, of course, one never does. Life changes.

## CHAPTER 8

# Arguments

We rarely argued. One of the reasons why was that Jose would shut down all communication if something was bothering him. This was extremely disturbing to me because often I wouldn't know what was wrong. And it might go on for two or three days. I was miserable. Then, just as quickly as it came on, the episode would be over. Even then, I didn't necessarily know what caused (or fixed) it.

Years later I realized that this was Jose's way of avoiding an argument that he would have had to pursue in his second language. He knew he would be at a disadvantage to try to express himself. He often stumbled over his words. And we joked about it. But I knew he didn't feel that he was on solid ground when it came to any emotionally charged discussion in English.

After having been together for many years, both of us knew when an argument was approaching. Most couples learn to recognize those moments. We were in one of those moments when Jose said something touching. He put his hand on my shoulder and said, "Ed, we're too old to do this." It was his sweet way of expressing, *We know where this is going, and there's no point in putting harsh words into a situation that in the end doesn't really matter that much.* Another way to put it is, why not just say "Okay" to your partner unless the magnitude of the circumstances demands more. Really, the majority of the time "Okay" works. I learned that to go with the flow makes everyone feel just fine almost all of the time. In the long run, neither one of us felt that the other one had the upper hand.

CHAPTER 9

# Painful Separation

Something happened in late 1985. I had resigned from the New Museum, thinking that I would be able to find a job in the foundation world if I put forth a reasonable amount of effort into a job search. After all, I had two relevant advanced degrees and a number of years of experience in the nonprofit sector.

But then things changed between Jose and me. Suddenly he became distant. Communication was minimal at best. He would turn away from me at night in bed. He was irritable, and came home later than usual. I knew something was very wrong. Strangely, one night he began to scrub the coffeepot vigorously and blamed me for not keeping it clean. To say the least, this was uncharacteristic. It was as though he were searching for reasons to justify what was inexplicably happening: we were coming apart.

Panicking, I went straight into denial. I told myself Jose was simply very stressed out from his work—which he was.

**Our tiny apartment on East 66th Street, late 1980s**

But truly I was aware that something, or *someone*, had come between us. After several weeks of this agonizing emotional distance, Jose left without a word one evening and didn't arrive back home until 2:00 a.m. It happened to be our fifth anniversary. I had been frantic, fearing that something awful had happened to him. I was crying. He didn't bother to offer any explanation. Most people would have divorced at that point.

A few nights later, after our friends Maury and Laurie dropped by for a short visit, Jose stopped what he was doing and said, "I have been seeing someone else."

I was both stunned and relieved. "Is this a problem your parents had?" I asked, thinking it might be a familiar pattern of behavior and trying to make sense of what was happening.

"No," he said, "I was pursued and pursued."

"We're *all* pursued," I said, meaning particularly gay guys. It's part of the game. It was, and perhaps still is, part of the gay lifestyle for many, though I would like to think that more and more gay couples nowadays find a way to stay committed in the long run, including marriage.

In any case, it was unbearable for me to remain in the apartment at that moment, sharing very close quarters. So I said, "I'm going out." It was a horrible night. Shell-shocked, I didn't feel like calling any friends. I had very little money, so I wandered over to an awful hotel on West Thirty-Fourth Street, where I lay down in a very spare room but slept very little.

The next day, feeling that I had to connect with some-one, I went to my friend Gail's apartment on East Fifty-Sixth Street to share what had happened. Gail was a sympathetic soul, and without hesitation generously invited me to stay with her in her small studio apartment. I felt both grateful and numb. I was afloat—not wanting to go back to our apart-ment, but needing someplace to hang onto.

I stayed with Gail for several days, returning to my apart-ment only to get the mail, desperately hoping not to see Jose. Next, I transferred to another kind friend's apartment in the Village, where I had more space. The host, Ellen, trav-eled frequently, so I could camp out more easily. Ellen and I had started our internships at the New Museum at the same time. Our backgrounds were very different. She had just gone through a divorce, and was well off financially and in middle age. She was feisty, musical, and independent—and still some-what bitter about her divorce. I was an impoverished graduate student when we first met, but we quickly found common interests and passions and had developed a strong friendship.

Other than confiding in Gail and Ellen, I kept all of these troubling developments to myself. I didn't mention them to anyone at work, where I had just started a new job—finally in the foundation world at MetLife. I continued my regular Sunday calls to my parents, but now from a random pay phone, typically in Chelsea or the Village. They must have suspected something wasn't right, but they didn't raise any questions.

Jose began to call me at work, asking if I was all right. It was excruciating. I got so choked up, I couldn't speak. I'm sure he misinterpreted it as bitterness and my determination to close off communication. Somehow we made a date to have dinner at a Thai restaurant in our old neighborhood on West Twenty-Second Street, just around the corner from where we spent our first magical year.

When we sat down at the restaurant, I asked Jose if he was absolutely certain that it was over between us.

"Yes," he said calmly.

After all those horrible weeks, crushing reality set in. I jumped up and ran out of the restaurant. Later, Ellen told me that Jose had called her, fearing I was suicidal. As a matter of fact, that wasn't out of the question.

In the following days, he continued to call at work. I was paralyzed.

One day Jose showed up at the office. Our secretary said that he was waiting in the lobby. This was in the headquarters building of MetLife, at One Madison Avenue. I had no idea what to expect, but I nervously walked out to meet him. Right away, we walked across the street to Madison Square Park, where we could talk privately. The moment we set foot in the park, Jose burst into tears. I was stunned. I never had seen him cry.

"I've made a mistake," he said.

I put my hand on his back but didn't say anything in response. Finally, after he talked more about his wrongheaded choice, I told him I would have to think about all of this. We parted with a ray of hope.

I had already searched, painfully but determinedly, for a new apartment of my own. I was financially and psychologically prepared to make a move to a single, independent life.

Jose, carrying a bouquet of flowers, began to show up at Ellen's apartment. I clearly remember the first one was yellow tulips. He was very hesitant, not wanting to appear presumptuous. I was cautious, feeling nearly mortally wounded. We would talk briefly at the front door. Flowers were given over, and then he would leave.

No games were being played. We were both trying to find a way back to our partnership. Two or three months went by in a kind of renewal courtship. I weighed the possibility of betrayal reoccurring and the devastation it would bring. But I also recognized the emotional risks we must all take in life. I honestly thought that Jose and I had a uniquely enduring bond, based on five years of shared hardship, mutual support, much joy, and ever-expanding relationships with family and friends.

Ultimately I decided that we could move back together. Along with that decision was the mutual determination to find a country house for two reasons: (1) we needed a getaway from the intensity of the city; and (2) it was part of the trendy '80s—New Yorkers were staking out country houses all over the place.

And so we did it. In October 1987, we bought a mini-farm in Catskill, New York. Some would have seen it as an old farmhouse that needed much repair. Others saw it as a bucolic little farm on Catskill Creek with an orchard, a little barn, and a creek house—perfect for evening barbeques and hammock lounging. Both impressions were correct.

The two of us spent weeks scraping old linoleum off wooden plank floors and attending local auctions where Jose, in his enthusiastic way, waved the bidder's paddle so excitedly that the auctioneer would need to say, "Sir, I already have your

The two of us with Roy on the creek in our back yard in Catskill, NY

bid." Typically, Jose would offer an embarrassed grin and then start all over with another auction piece.

It was hard work but great fun making a tired old house into an inviting home where we hosted many New York City guests and several family visits from both sides, including the Joneses' 1987 Christmas. During family visits, Jose slept on the porch. I would go to him so we could spend private time together when everyone else was upstairs. Eventually, times changed, and we didn't bother with separateness, whether it was at family homes or hotels.

I should be honest about this earlier, painful separation period. It was cause for lingering doubts for the rest of our years together. But I consciously made a trade-off. I could

Jose with my sister, Fluffy. c. 1988

make a new start with the partner I wanted to share all of life's challenges and pleasures with, or I could start a very different life without him. It was clear to me that I preferred to share life (flawed as it might be) with Jose rather than chart a new course.

As this played out, we forged a solid bond, even greater than before in many ways. But the doubts and emotional scars would never completely go away. And there were later indiscretions by both parties—unspoken and unacknowledged. There was always an excuse to act out, based on the pain the split-up had caused. In a way, we were protecting one another *and* protecting our partnership. The new shared experiences and the words that *were* spoken always played out against a backdrop of permanency. The mutual assumption was that we were staying together. Period.

Some would say that this was a dishonest situation, even fraudulent. I would admit to some dishonesty, even deception. But it was the life we chose—flawed, but fully loving and committed in our way. Again, we protected one another. And we respected one another and the life we had made together with all of the interconnectedness of family, friends, hardships, excitement, sadness, and affection. If an apology for deception is called for, I apologize to any friends and family that feel deceived. But know that what you observed was genuine. The bond and the love were quite real. And after Jose was gone, I would often say this mantra for both of us: "I forgive you, and you forgive me."

CHAPTER 10

# Private Moments

J ose and I would often hold hands, but throughout most of our time together, holding hands in public would have invited others' reactions that we didn't want to face. Activists we were not. So we held hands in private. That made it sweeter in a way. But it's wonderful to now see gay couples be openly affectionate.

In the theater—and we went often because of my job— we would hold hands just as the lights went down. Or I would slide my hand under his leg and just let it rest there. Meanwhile, I would have to poke him if I saw that he was dozing off—a frequent possibility due to his long work hours. Otherwise he'd start to snore, which embarrassingly happened a few times.

We held hands in taxicabs. Just sitting next to one another, it was a very natural thing. And in taxicabs, Jose wouldn't hesitate to give detailed directions, sometimes to the frustration of the driver. Jose had total recall of every street he had ever been on. And having worked in all five boroughs of New York, he knew many, many streets.

In twenty-one years, I saw Jose cry only three times. He had great emotional strength, or at least emotional control. The first instance was when he showed up at my office during our separation.

The second instance was when his father passed away. He wasn't sobbing, but I looked over at him as we sat together in the funeral chapel and saw tears running down his face. On top of the emotional drain of having his father gradually fade away, Jose had to be in and out of his clinical mode. He would distance himself as son, and then as an MD analyze the illnesses that his father suffered. Afterward he would convey

Jose, the natural-born pediatrician

any "clinical" messages to his brothers and sisters. Most impressively, when his father had taken a turn for the worse and was in the hospital hooked up to numerous tubes and machines, Jose very calmly, capably, and sensitively explained to all of his siblings, seated in a circle in the hospital lobby, that their father was in a very critical situation and decisions had to be made about perpetuating his life support or not. He was very mindful that his brothers and sisters probably were not in agreement on this difficult issue, but he wanted to convey the facts as he saw them. My tremendous respect for him grew even greater that day.

The third instance I observed came one morning out of the blue as we were dressing for work. Jose was sitting on his little stool where he kept his prosthetic socks. I was stunned to

Jose in his natural mode with nephew, Connor

see him crying. This never happened. "Jose, what's wrong?" I asked. He explained that he was thinking about the mother of some of his little patients at the hospital. Apparently she was a hardworking, very caring mother, who probably reminded him of his own mother in some ways. He was crying about her selflessness as a mother, and probably her total dedication to her children as she navigated through a very difficult life with strength and dignity and determination, all of which were qualities Jose inherited from his parents.

CHAPTER 11

# Traveling

In the summer of 1999, our vacation was planned in conjunction with Jose's family. His sister Chato had taken on a monumental (crazy?) task of renting a van and driving throughout Europe with her three children and her aging parents. One of the many things Jose and his sister had in common was determination. Absolute determination! They also shared a great sense of joy about life, and both were quick to laugh in a wonderfully uninhibited way—often leaving the rest of us wondering what was so hysterically funny. Often we never found out.

Jose had long since decided to let family trips take their course. He had learned that throughout the years in a big family (especially in a big Filipino family) plans were always changing and people didn't always agree. So we set out on our own to meet Chato and family initially in Siena and then later crossed paths with them in Nice.

Actually, there was a method to Chato's madness. She had

carefully charted out her route based on the series of travel books by Rick Steves. And she had taken pains to make arrangements with guesthouses in the many cities along the route. Her older son, Ryan, who at the time was about twelve years old, would navigate quite capably. A few times Jose's dad would threaten to fly back home after he realized that this was another "death march," having survived the Bataan Death March in the Philippines in World War II. He had emphysema and struggled with the stairs at the guesthouses and during many walks in the towns they visited.

Jose and I arrived in Siena, where we had visited once before. We settled into a comfortable little hotel in the center of the city not far from the cathedral. We had dinner and a stroll around town in the evening before retiring. The next morning I volunteered to go out and bring breakfast back to the hotel. This was a routine that I enjoyed in New York on weekends. I was happy to let Jose rest and relax and not put on his leg until it was time to go outside.

As I walked down the narrow, ancient cobblestone road toward the market, looking around for a breakfast that was portable and acceptable to Americans, I heard someone shout my name. I couldn't imagine who could possibly know me in Siena. I turned around and saw Jose's dad standing there, smiling.[1] We had a good laugh about the coincidence and

---

1  During my many years with Jose, I enjoyed having a beer with his dad. He reminded me of my father in many ways. They were from opposite sides of the world, but they were born in the same year and were both keenly interested in history and jovial by nature. I wish they had met one another. They could have been great pals. They died one month apart.

planned to meet up later in the day for a joint outing.

The decision was made to travel together in our two rented cars down to Assisi. It was a stunning drive through Umbria. And the group (ages eight to eighty) thoroughly enjoyed taking in this beautiful part of the world and absorbing the rich Italian culture. We stopped for lunch at a restaurant overlooking the picturesque valley, which was quintessentially Italian. Later, at Assisi, Jose's mom decided to walk up the long hill to the chapel, a major tourist destination. Jose's dad was not up to it and sat on a bench at the bottom of the hill, pouting with his arms folded. He was not happy that everyone was leaving him by himself. Jose, in his usual thoughtful way, had bought an atomizer for his dad in case he had a bad spell with his breathing. On our way back, his dad threatened once again to leave the group and return to California. After fifty years of marriage, Jose's mom knew how to deal with that. She basically ignored him.

**With Jose's family near Assisi**

After Siena, we parted ways. Jose and I took off for Cinque Terra—five small towns on the gorgeous Italian Riviera. It was a beautiful drive up the lush, green coast of the Ligurian Sea. As we approached Monterosso, the first town where we had a hotel reservation, we realized that half of the population of Italy had spent the weekend at Cinque Terra, and they were departing that Sunday afternoon en masse. This tiny village had a gigantic parking lot, where police were directing traffic. Our little rental car had to hug the side of a cliff to let the buses coming from the opposite direction pass. As we reached the parking lot, we were told that we must park the car there and take a taxi to the hotel.

It was the wildest taxi ride we had ever taken, including the frequent eye-popping taxi rides in New York City. The driver, who seemed to know exactly what he was doing, plowed through the masses of people strolling on the sidewalks and very narrow lanes. I looked to the side, not to see pedestrians ahead whom we might soon be murdering with the car. As we got closer to the hotel, the lanes got narrower and narrower so that we could barely pass through ancient archways that were obviously built for primitive carts, not modern automobiles. Then at the end of the ride it seemed that the driver was going to drive up the stone stairs at the hotel, but thankfully he paused.

Once inside the hotel, or bed and breakfast, we were greeted at the desk by a beautiful young woman who resembled Sophia Loren. We gave her our information, and she carefully searched through the reservation book. Soon we learned that the reservation had been made (by Jose) for the following day! (I had long since learned not to say a word of complaint because the next mistake might very well be mine.) In any case, "young Sophia Loren," who had been so pleasant and helpful, told us that the owners were on a family picnic nearby and would return shortly. "Sophia Loren" didn't even work there. She was a guest! It's Italy. People just do these things.

Shortly, the owners returned, and another extraordinary young woman took charge. She was not at all disturbed that we had no reservation for the first night. She said that she could accommodate us in their home, which was adjacent to the hotel. We gladly agreed to the arrangement. She took us to the room; made the bed; gave us a tour of the hotel; gave instructions to the staff; and hopped on her motorcycle and sped away. Wow! We were impressed!

Cinque Terre was a destination for hikers. The five little towns were just close enough for a challenging but doable hike. And they were perfectly spaced so that hikers could pause in each village for a meal overlooking the sea, or they could stay the night and hike the next day. Because of Jose's disability, we took the train instead. And as we waited on the platform in Monterosso, we struck up a conversation with two young American women who were also exploring Cinque Terre by train. We spent the day with them, having lunch and hopping from Vernazza to Corniglia to Manarola to Riomaggiore, and then back to Monterosso. All the while, Jose was in touch with his sister, who would be following us to Cinque Terre with her kids and parents in a few days. We would meet up with them in Nice.

**Italy 1990s**

Nice has a wonderful balance between a big city and a laid-back Mediterranean feel to it. We arrived at our charming little boutique hotel. The proprietress greeted us and explained that parking was very limited. She showed us to the designated parking space behind the hotel, where Jose prepared to park our rental car. Ordinarily he was fine with parking, having had much practice in New York with challenging parking spots. But this particular situation was different. After several tries, Madame said to Jose, "Monsieur, I will park your car." And she did so, promptly. Jose was irked.

Other major trips involved each of our fiftieth birthdays. Mine came first. In January 1997, Jose said, "Pack for a warm climate." He wouldn't say where we were going. I don't remember exactly when the destination was revealed, but we set off to a magical island in the Grenadines just north of Venezuela in the Caribbean called Petit St. Vincent. Jose loved surprises and he loved luxury. This was a fabulous destination and a perfect getaway from the harsh winter in New York.

On the island, there were no phones or cars, just endless beautiful beaches and cozy cottages—all part of the resort owned by a man who had bought and developed the island. If you wanted a picnic delivered to your cottage, or if you wanted to be transported to one of the beaches, you only needed to raise the appropriate flag, and soon one of the staff members would arrive in a golf cart and off you would go. On my birthday, Jose hired a local sailor to take us out in his yacht for snorkeling and feasting in some of the nearby reefs. As we returned, the sun was setting on the horizon and simultaneously the moon was rising. Perfection! This was Jose's over-the-top way of pampering me. We both loved it.

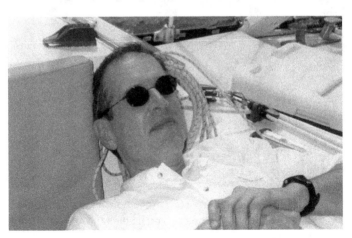

Enjoying my 50th birthday cruise

Not to be outdone, I made arrangements to celebrate his fiftieth birthday four years later, in December 2000. After researching destinations in the Caribbean, a destination we both preferred in the wintertime, I settled on Mustique, a private island also in the Grenadines. Like Jose, I also kept the destination a secret until the last minute.

We flew to Barbados and then took a puddle jumper to Mustique. We landed in the "airport" at dusk. It looked more like a cleared piece of land in a lush botanical garden. I don't recall any pavement, just grass. A driver was waiting for us in a Jeep that would be at our disposal for the week. When he delivered us to our destination, a woman with a beaming smile and in a colorful dress was waiting for us on the steps,

In the kitchen with the house staff in the house I rented on the island of Mustique. After they served us dinner, we would hang out with them in the kitchen.

drinks in hand. You could immediately see the sea beyond the main room just ahead.

"Ed, what a beautiful hotel!" Jose said.

"Jose, this is our *house* for a week."

His disbelief made the whole trip worthwhile.

On his actual birthday, I arranged an excursion with the same sailor who had taken us on my birthday voyage four years earlier, in Petit St. Vincent. But the sailor's boat range was limited. We would have to meet him halfway, on Union Island, which held a tiny airport.

I chartered a four-seater plane to take us there, not telling Jose what to expect. After about a ten-minute flight, we had a very precarious and jarring landing. That explained why we had two pilots. One was in training; he had been at the controls. Perhaps it was his first attempt at that airport. Later we learned that the locals called him Billy the Skid.

After a short walk from the airport to the seaside, we were greeted by Jeff, the same skipper who had taken us on my birthday voyage four years earlier. Jose was blown away, and that made me very happy.

## CHAPTER 12

# Long Island Life

In the summer of 1996, Jose and I were planning a day trip out on Long Island—perhaps going to the Hamptons or all the way to Montauk. When I mentioned this trip to our friends Steve and Anne Dennin, they invited us to stop by their place in Bellport on the way back to Manhattan. We hadn't been to Bellport and probably had never heard of it. Bellport is a sleepy little village on the Great South Bay of Long Island just across from Fire Island, only one and a half hours from New York City. It's a well-kept secret. Other than learning that the Dennins had had a "barn" there for many years, we had no idea what to expect.

Steve and Anne greeted us at their comfortable garage apartment, which seemed more like a miniloft overlooking the Great South Bay. It felt like one of those places meant for slow, easy dinners with fresh seafood and plenty of wine. They gave us a quick tour of this magical-looking village with its wonderful mix of solidly grounded liberal political locals, gay weekenders, and summer renters. Compared to the quaint town of Catskill, where we had our previous country house, it was conveniently close to home. Catskill was wonderful in many respects, but it was far away, and maintaining an 1870s farmhouse with more than three acres of land was sometimes more hard work than a welcome escape to recharge.

Bellport offered an enticing retreat. The commute was short, making for an easy getaway. It was a natural decision to look at renting a place for the next summer, in 1997. We found a tiny cottage, barely big enough for a bed in a "bedroom." But it had a wonderful little porch overlooking the bay and a landlady who would march up her sidewalk in the morning toward our porch and give us the day's weather report without breaking her stride. She was close to ninety and drove a red sports car.

That little cottage was the beginning of a home base for us in Bellport.

We were introduced to a real estate agent, Annie, who stayed in touch and showed us many houses—most of which were rather conventional and boring. One of them was a very attractive "Cape" with a wonderful, spacious feeling—a two-story cottage with double-size bedrooms, French doors, and an ample yard and trees. But when we explored the basement, I ran out in a panic.

"What's wrong?" Annie asked.

I explained that the basement reminded me of all the things that went wrong with our house in Catskill. Call it basement phobia.

We continued our search for a piece of property to make

our own. Later, Annie called with a prospect on a little road farther east in the village in a neighborhood where a developer had built tract houses on three short roads in about 1950. It wasn't the quaint village look we'd envisioned, but more a mix of bungalow/suburban/Miami Beach style. Realtors disparagingly referred to the neighborhood as "Alcatraz" because the houses were constructed of concrete and masonry.

The available house was a plain two-bedroom structure with very outdated interior design and a hanging extension cord in the kitchen that served all appliances, including a washing machine accessible through a hole in the kitchen counter. It was a mess, but affordable and easy to maintain!

After several rounds of negotiation, we were close to an agreeable price, which in retrospect was a fraction of its value a few years later. Finally Annie said, "You should decide. There are others interested who are bidding higher than you!" So we signed the deal.

Later we met the two guys who were bidding against us. They became our next-door neighbors because they soon bought the next available house. And they quickly became good friends. We had only expected a weekend getaway close to the city, never even hoping for a gay-friendly village.

Jose loved to do two things in Bellport: cook and relax. Having a full-size kitchen was heaven for him. And when he cooked (always without a recipe), he used most of the pots and pans in the kitchen. But for me, it was worth the cleanup. His cooking was fabulous. He would always offer the cooking spoon and ask me to taste whatever he was making, including his version of chicken soup with a whole chicken, potatoes, carrots, celery, lots of garlic, and all sorts of greens and spices; many Filipino dishes; and later, some adapted French country recipes. His other great pleasure was to take long naps in the afternoon. I would do yard work or housework.

Often in the evenings we would take walks in the village—especially if we could pass by Carla Marla's Ice Cream Parlor. Then we would head down to Bellport's village marina, where we would admire the boats and dream about the time when we would have our own boat slip there. The village marina is beautiful on a summer evening. The moon shines over Great South Bay, and if it's bright enough you can see Fire Island in the distance.

A ferry shuttles locals and summer renters back and forth all day to Ho-Hum Beach. Unlike much of Fire Island, where

Our last Christmas, December, 2001. My mother, sister and aunt Mary Frances came up from Texas. My father had passed away that year and Jose would be gone in 2½ months.

you'll find charming or funky houses, depending on the community, Ho-Hum Beach consists of only a concession stand, plenty of clean sand, and a couple of lifeguards on duty. That's it. We would spend time on the beach with both gay and straight friends, depending on who showed up. Back at the house, we enjoyed hosting occasional small dinner parties and family gatherings.

Jose's parents, brothers and sisters, and nieces and nephews came to enjoy Bellport. In 2000, two of our nephews, Justin and Joseph, spent the summer with us. We loved being surrogate parents for a short time. Jose was perfect in that role. As a pediatrician and a member of a huge family, he always knew just the right thing to say to teenagers, whether it was encouraging them to have fun, disciplining them if necessary,

Jose, Justin and Joseph on Fire Island beach near Bellport

or just offering good advice. I was admittedly clueless in that role, but I enjoyed every minute of being a "coparent."

On one occasion, Justin, Joseph, and Noel (another nephew, who was visiting from New Jersey) were headed to the beach. We didn't feel like going with them that day, but I did want to be a responsible "parent." So in the living room of our house, before they took the ferry by themselves, I asked them to raise their right hand and swear, "I promise to be careful and to swim only between the red flags where the lifeguards are watching us."

Two short years later, when Jose was gone, Justin (by then a very wise and mature eighteen-year-old) came to live with me. That was the result of a promise we had made to him when he announced in high school that he wanted to move to New York, live with us, and attend college. I was thrilled! Jose was anxious. It turned out to be one of the best things that ever happened to me.

After Jose passed away, we stuck to the plan. I flew to California for Justin's graduation and brought him back to New York. Initially, he entered Lower Manhattan Community College. The three of us had agreed that a community college might be the best way for him to make the transition from his particular local school system in Fort Bragg, California, to an intense, urban environment. But it became obvious that he was capable of achieving far more than what the community college offered. After one semester, he transferred to Hunter College, on the East Side of Manhattan.

Justin, a delightful, smart, thoughtful, caring young man, so wise for his years and often the adult in the room (when

**Fluffy and Kathy's house. Justin is on the left.**

I was among those in the room), was my saving grace in the difficult years immediately after Jose's passing. I was so proud to introduce him as my nephew. Everyone who met him wanted to take him home and care for him. I knew then, and I understand now, that it was a very difficult period for Justin too. Despite tremendous support from many friends and family often visiting, his Uncle Ed was in a deep depression. Meanwhile, Justin did exceedingly well at Hunter College, where he studied anthropology and media.

I felt responsible for him—this young guy who wasn't quite yet an adult in the big city. One of my house rules was that he could stay out as late as he wanted, but he must knock on my door when he got home so I would know he was home safe. Often, when he knocked on my door, I was still awake, and we would have great conversations about what was going on in school or life in general. I don't know what I would have done without Justin. Starting from the day Jose passed away, I was not alone for a single day for three years. I don't know how people survive otherwise.

CHAPTER 13

# A Partner Can Vanish

It was Friday evening, March 1, 2002. Fridays we would head out for our house on Long Island, just as many other New Yorkers head out for their country houses, weekend retreats, beach houses, or one-time getaways—the great Friday evening exodus. Often on Friday evenings I would call Jose from the gym and ask if he was almost finished at work. He was in the pediatrics department at Gouverneur Hospital on the Lower East Side in Manhattan. I worked at J. P. Morgan on Wall Street, not far from there. Most of the time he would say, "Yep, I'll be finished in twenty minutes." Thirty minutes later he would pull up on Water Street, headed in the direction of FDR Drive, and we would be on our way.

On this particular Friday, I asked him how he was feeling. Jose had had the flu for several days but recovered and went back to work the day before. He said that he still didn't feel great, so I decided we should stay at home in the city.

Over the weekend, Jose had a relapse. It wasn't so bad, just the same flu keeping him down. He had a way of minimizing his own illnesses, and often he would bounce back very quickly or get up and go out for supplies, ignoring his sickness. This was typical of him and so many other doctors. They truly are the worst patients.

Meanwhile, our good friend Joey Miranda, also a pediatrician from the Philippines, stopped by each day to bring soup and ask how things were going. Joey was Jose's best friend and the two shared so many things in common: gay, MD, Filipino immigrant to New York, and he lived just down the street—six blocks down Broadway. Since "Joey" was one of Jose's many nicknames, the two of them would call each other "Joey I" and "Joey II."

On Monday, Jose still felt lousy. I told him to rest up, and I went on to work. Late in the afternoon, Jose called me at work and asked me to bring home several things from the drugstore. Again, Joey Miranda came that evening. When Jose complained that he didn't eat all day, I asked what he was craving, and he said, "Popsicles." I went down to the market and bought three dozen Popsicles so he would have a good selection. After another conversation much like the last two nights, Joey asked Jose if he had any other symptoms. Jose said no. Joey II went home.

That night was bad. Jose was up several times with diarrhea. He had told me to sleep in the living room so I wouldn't catch his flu, but he would call out to me when he had to go so

I could carry him to the bathroom. The third or fourth time, I was asleep, but awoke as he was hopping back toward the bedroom. Alarmed, I called out, "Jose, wait! Let me carry you. You might fall." I picked him up again and took him back to bed. He was losing fluids and getting weaker.

In the morning he was exhausted but had no particular complaints. I told him to rest and that he should expect Joey to stop by midmorning. I kissed him good-bye and said that I had a breakfast meeting across town. One of my great regrets is that I didn't *say* that I planned to come back home after my meeting to check on him. Perhaps I thought he would tell me to stay at work.

At about 10:15 a.m., when I left the meeting with our department head and another foundation officer at the Palace Hotel, I told her I was going home because Jose was sicker than he had been in twenty years. When I got into the cab, I had a message on my cell phone to call my assistant, Janice. She told me that Jose had called her at work to say that he wanted me to come home. I told Janice that I was already on my way; then I called Jose to tell him.

When I arrived, Jose had developed a new and alarming symptom: he was very short of breath. I told him I was going to call an ambulance.

"We can just take the car," he said.

"No," I said. "They will be able to treat you in the ambulance."

Within fifteen minutes, possibly ten, the emergency medical team showed up. They brought the stretcher straight into the bedroom and did a great job of collecting information from me as they prepared Jose for the trip to the hospital. In my anxiety I became impatient; I wanted to move ahead right away. This may have taken only five minutes, but it seemed much longer. As they rolled him out, I put his leg on the stretcher with him (this was my natural reaction after twenty-one years of being mindful of his false leg) and Jose told me to get his wallet out of his pants so he would have it with him.

Once we were in the ambulance, I sat behind him. I was strapped in, but I could just reach far enough to place my hand on his forehead to comfort him. Although he now wore an oxygen mask, he was gasping for air and saying, "I can't breathe." I insisted that he keep the mask on. What else should we have done? At the time I thought he mainly needed fluids to replace what he had lost the night before.

In the ambulance, Jose asked to be taken to St. Vincent's Hospital in Greenwich Village. We arrived there very quickly. The emergency team had done an excellent job from the get-go. They took him straight into the emergency room, where the staff began to work on him immediately. There was a curtain around Jose's bed. I reached through the curtain, put my hand on his shoulder, and said, "Jose, I'm right here." Those were the last words Jose heard me say. The nurses sent me out, saying that I couldn't stay there.

Panic was setting in. I went to the sidewalk and tried calling Jose's personal doctor. He said that there wasn't anything he could do that the emergency room staff wasn't already doing. I left a message with Joey Miranda, saying, "This is extreme."

I returned to the emergency room again and again, each time being sent out by the staff. On the third try, Jose seemed to be resting peacefully. Then, on my next return, I was greeted by one of the nurses or doctors, I don't know exactly. He had a sympathetic smile on his face, and he said, "He didn't make it." I couldn't believe his words, but the words had their own stark reality. I began to scream, "No!" I remember holding my hands to the sides of my face, very similar to the figure in Edvard Munch's painting *The Scream*. I believe I turned in each direction, continuing to scream as though I might have been seeking some alternative reality in another direction. I couldn't stop. I didn't want to look in the direction of Jose's bed, confirming what was happening. Finally, probably thinking I might faint, the doctor told me to sit down.

I don't think anyone working in the emergency room that day will ever forget my screams. I had never fully, totally screamed before or after that day. It was primal, out of the horror of the moment.

Right away I was taken to a grim little room with a small table and a telephone where I proceeded to call as many family members as I could. First Chato, Jose's sister and soul mate. I was breathing heavily and couldn't get out a complete sentence.

"Chato, I have the worst news in the world," I said. Panting, I tried to get the words out. "Jose has passed away."

"What?!" Naturally, she was in disbelief.

I tried to explain. She had known that he had the flu, but no one had any reason to believe that it was a particularly serious case or anything out of the ordinary. I don't recall the rest of the conversation, but I know that she then called the rest of the family. I tried to call others but didn't reach many. I tried to reach Jose's cousin Reggie in Brooklyn. The two were very close. I did reach her father-in-law. We were all concerned about Reggie receiving the news, as she was pregnant.

I called my sister, saying, "I need you now more than I ever have." Not surprisingly, she rose to the occasion and showed up the next day along with her partner, Kathy. They were, and still are, a wonderful couple, devoted to each other as well as to family and friends. They took care of me for a number of days, through and after the funeral. Fluffy offered to stay in my room, but I said that I would be all right. I was far from all right.

I'll never find the words that adequately describe the

Jose and his cousin Reggie when we took a drive in Connecticut. Jose tended to dress up.

sudden loss of a life partner. He simply vanished! From a lively, childlike glowing presence in the world to an instantaneous absence. Later, one of my several counselors and psychiatrists asked how much of myself I felt as though I had lost. Without hesitating I said, "Fifty percent." Half of me was gone.

In the first number of days, I had the distinct feeling that Jose was present in our bedroom, in a fetal position, hovering over our doorway. It seemed that he was silently watching over me. I was numb. I would sob uncontrollably and then stop myself out of a fear of what would come next after the sobbing. It was an unknown state of mind that I feared. I feared going to sleep, not knowing what hellish dreams might come into my mind, and I dreaded waking up into the living nightmare of my new reality.

Jose's entire family was present at the funeral, which took place in the Great Choir of the enormous Cathedral Church of St. John the Divine, a short distance from our apartment. Just over two months prior, Jose and I had attended the New Year's concert there, never dreaming that his funeral would take place in that grand structure in the near future.

Jose's mother was seated next to me. She had lost her husband, Jose's father, only ten months before. I had long since called her Mom. She was a petite, thin, soft-spoken lady. Her appearance was deceiving. I've never met a stronger person. It's always been clear to me where Jose got his unwavering determination. And if she ever expressed a need or a desire for something in particular, one or all of her children would jump to see that she got it, practically before the words left her mouth.

I will be eternally grateful to her for staying with me for the two weeks following Jose's funeral, along with one of our nieces, the wonderful, sweet Christina. And again, my sister stayed for a number of days as well. I honestly can't comprehend someone enduring the same circumstances without family members. But so many people do. It was only the year before, when my father passed away, that I watched my mother survive the loss of her husband of almost sixty years. After the funeral, all of the well-wishers went home. How my mother and millions of others endure the next weeks and months without family in the house is something I could not have endured, certainly not in any remotely intact mental state. I stayed with my mother for a few days after the funeral, but in retrospect it should have been longer.

Jose's sister Chato also remained with her children for several days after the funeral. As she left for California, she said, "If you need me, just call." Approximately two weeks went by. I was in a terrible state of mind, not knowing how to get from one day to the next. I called Chato and said, "I need you." She arrived the next day with all three kids. What more do I need to say about her? I wouldn't have survived in any reasonably normal condition without my sister, Jose's mom, Christina, and Chato. Numerous other friends formed the greatest support group anyone could have asked for, taking calls from me at all hours of the day and night, and just showing up. One only needs to be present and listen to be a great help.

Very soon after Jose passed away, the medical examiner gave us her preliminary opinion about the cause of death: asymptomatic heart disease. This came as a surprise, as I hadn't known of any heart problems in Jose's past. But it partly explained why his death was so sudden after what seemed to be a normal case of the flu with a relapse.

A few days later, Joey Miranda and I met with the medical examiner for her full report. Joey was Jose's best friend and an MD himself. She stated up front that Jose had HIV. I was stunned and confused. She proceeded to go through a detailed, clinical explanation of the many things she had found. After the first few minutes, I had to leave the room. It was unbearable to learn about all of the major health problems he had. How could he have lived so normally until just a few days prior? Had Jose known he was HIV positive? After all, he was an MD and had significant experience with HIV patients.

If he knew, he never mentioned it to me. Was he in denial? It's possible. It's also possible that he contracted HIV at his job in a New York City STD clinic where he drew blood from HIV patients. As far as I know, he was never tested for HIV himself. I mentioned this to one of his brothers. Then I suppose the rest of the family eventually learned it from him. Jose was more complicated than many people realized. We will never know the answer to these questions. As for myself, I was suddenly concerned about my own HIV status. But soon I would be tested. The result was negative.

Some of the most loving, sincere, heartwarming condolences came from highly traditional, conservative, octogenarian friends of my parents. They knew a genuine, enduring relationship when they saw it. And we had it. One comment came from my mother's lifelong friend and next-door neighbor, Jane. She was a well-to-do, talented, well-read, well-traveled, but sometimes ultraconservative housewife. Her comment about us was, "They were a model couple." What an astonishing thing for me to hear!

Similar statements came from other local older generation friends who had come to know Jose and me as a couple. I have to think that we made an impression. Not because we would flagrantly cling to each other, but because we didn't. Because we consistently treated each other with respect, consideration, humor, and affection, just as they would have expected an enduring straight relationship to be. Meanwhile, at their advanced age, they had come to learn that a large segment of the straight population had trouble maintaining relationships—all the more reason to recognize an authentic partnership when they saw it!

As I've stated before, humor was never far from Jose. As executor of his estate, I plunged into his scattered files—not an easy task, as there was no rhyme or reason to his filing methods. One critical piece was his safety deposit box at the bank. Jose was a pack rat, so in addition to whatever mystery there was around his death, I was very anxious to find out about the contents of the box at the bank. And as his executor, it was part of my responsibility.

I searched for the key everywhere, with no luck. So after arranging for the lock to be drilled out, my niece Christina and I went to the bank for the inevitable opening. Christina was looking after me at the time. She was a natural-born

Combined families at Jose's funeral, March 9, 2002, at the
Cathedral St. John the Divine, New York City

lifesaver. I was full of anxiety and, as was always the case in
those days, just a hair trigger away from tears. We were shown
into a private room. The lock was drilled. The moment came.
I shakily lifted the top of the box, expecting it to be bulg-
ing with surprises, some of which I may not have wanted to
know about.

There was one small item—an expired international driver's license. Christina and I looked at each other and burst out
in laughter. I'm sure the loudest laugh in the room was from
Jose. His usual "Ha!" followed by giggles and uncontrolled
laughs as though he were saying, "See! You don't have to be so
sad. Go ahead and live!"

## CHAPTER 14

# My Thoughts on Jose

On the first anniversary of his death, I prepared this short piece about Jose to be read to the family in the chapel at the cathedral where he was entombed. I wasn't able to read it. I stood next to Justin, who generously offered to read it for me.

> It's difficult to do justice to Jose in words, but this is what I will say about him today:
>
> We met as young men on January 2, 1981, and departed twenty-one years later on this date, as middle-aged men. But age really had nothing to do with Jose's great spirit, which was exuberant and childlike.
>
> Jose was a loving and devoted son, brother, uncle, friend, and life partner. He was a dedicated pediatrician who took delight in the successes of his young

patients—especially as they progressed through their education. In turn, they and their parents were devoted to him.

He will be remembered as a person full of laughter. He wasn't large in size, but gigantic in spirit and determination. Quick to help anyone in need, but never complaining about his own handicap.

He engaged just about anyone in conversation, and always left them with a smile on their face—occasionally a quizzical smile because of his wonderful, quirky way with words. It was part of his enormous charm.

Jose's absence has left a tremendous hole in our lives. But he would have wanted us to come closer together and fill that hole. He would have wanted us to look forward and focus our energy on the next generation.

I have a profound sadness now, but I will try to move toward the happiness that he would have wanted and that he personified. We will do that together—this family of ours.

Now, as I said to him every morning just as I helped him out of the shower to get ready for the new day, "Jose, I love you always, always, always."

—Ed

Handsome guy

Jose on our way to Ellis Island where he would be sworn in as a new U.S. citizen by the Chief Justice, 1986.

# Seven Dreams

In the days and weeks following Jose's passing, I had a number of dreams about him. These were the most vivid dreams I've ever had before or since. I believe they were sent from another place.

## DREAM 1—APRIL 14, 2002

Jose and I were in a dark, spacious room—perhaps a set of rooms or an apartment. I don't recall any furniture, but there may have been some. The only other person present was a middle-aged woman with honey-colored hair. She may have had a German accent or some other accent. She wasn't especially attractive or unattractive, but she was serious, though not stern. She directed us to a large trap door in the floor. The door opened, and we proceeded down some steps. We weren't afraid, but we didn't know what was ahead. We entered another place somewhat similar to the first, where somehow we were made to feel that it was a place for us to stay (indefinitely). I don't recall that either Jose or I said anything; we just felt that this was our place. I then looked up and could see the sky all around. It seemed to be another universe. We remained in our place.

## DREAM 2—JULY 31, 2002

An old song, "When Your Lover Has Gone," was playing over and over in my head. I was tossing and turning because the song was bothersome. Ironically, the sound of the music was that of a big band—lush, full and first-rate. Jose appeared in the distance. He was dressed in a familiar suit and bow tie. He had the biggest smile, full of excitement, energy, and joy. He gestured for me to join him and dance.

*When you're alone, who cares for starlit skies*
*When you're alone, the magic moonlight dies*
*At break of dawn, there is no sunrise*
*When your lover has gone*

## DREAM 3—FEBRUARY 23, 2003

This was the first dream I had about Jose in many months. After the first two vivid dreams were sent to me, there had been nothing else—all the more reason to believe they were special messages. Meanwhile, I thought it was strange that the person who was on my mind all day long every day, didn't appear in my dreams.

However, last night Jose was there. His appearance was the same except that the hair on the top of his head was either trimmed very short or becoming very thin. Otherwise, he looked healthy and happy and calm. I believe he was carrying a small bag—probably his usual backpack or a shoulder bag. I knew that he was there only for the evening, and he would have to leave. We were in a large house or inn with big spacious rooms for all of his family. We were all in a very large living room. It seemed to be all on one floor, which was always better for Jose because of his leg, and it was all white. The interior was very nicely finished with refined, but understated fixtures, windows, and doors. Jose was distracted by his family, and I was frustrated that we couldn't get together alone. Later, I think we were sleeping on the floor together, but only briefly. Chato was there and I was glad to see her, but wanted to spend time with Jose alone, knowing that he would have to be leaving soon. I walked outside hoping that I could return to find him alone. Chato was outside picking flowers. I went back into the house and Jose was playing with some of the youngest nephews—probably Tino and Francis. He looked at me as though he wanted to join me, but felt he needed to stay with Tino and Francis at the moment. The dream ended.

## DREAM 4—MAY 6, 2003

This was only the fourth dream I've had about Jose since he passed away. In the dream, I woke up thinking I was late for an appointment. I went into the living room, and Jose was seated in a large bay window straight ahead. He was in his bathrobe eating breakfast and reading the paper. As usual, his leg was off since he hadn't showered yet. The house was a large two-story, very spacious place—not refined, but comfortable. The bay window behind Jose overlooked a huge green lawn sloping down in the distance as far as the eye could see. As I walked into the room, Jose stood up and we hugged each other. "I've missed you so much," I said. It felt so wonderful to hug him again. In a way, it seemed like a regular day. Jose said that there had been a big storm the night before and the power had gone off, so that was why I overslept. I then said that I should hurry up and get ready to go. I don't know if I had a sense of parting for a long time or just for the day. The dream ended. It was very comforting to have seen him. I wish he would come into my dream every night.

## DREAM 5—SEPTEMBER 15, 2003

Jose's appearance was very bad. He was clearly ill, but his family didn't seem to notice it. I was concerned that no one realized his severe illness. Later, I observed Jose lying in bed, perhaps reading, and with a light on the nightstand. At that point, he appeared very healthy. He had a content, happy expression on his face, and his skin was glowing—healthy, full of color and youthful. I believe I was approaching him, but I don't think we actually made contact. I think he was aware I was present.

## DREAM 6—MARCH 14, 2004

I had a brief dream of Jose last night. I was in the kitchen of our apartment on West 100th Street, and I was scrubbing some pans. Jose walked in the door with a beaming smile on his face, and he was carrying some very large trays. It was as though both of us had been somehow serving separate groups and now, at last, we were together alone. We hugged with that feeling in mind, but also with the feeling that this visit was for a brief period. I recognized one of the trays he was carrying. It had been in our family for as long as I can remember. My mother used it fairly often to serve food or drinks during parties. It was brass with a turquoise color base and fairly large—perhaps twenty inches across. The handles and some decorative circles were brass. The dream was comforting.

## DREAM 7—JANUARY 5, 2006

Jose and I were in a van that belonged to us. We were parked in the middle of First Avenue near our old apartment, which was on East 66th Street. The street had been blocked off for an event, so many cars were there. People were in their cars having picnics just as we were. Then we realized the event was over; we were the only car in the middle of First Avenue and traffic was zooming past us. We pulled over to the side of the road because we wanted to stay there. Jose might have had his leg off. We just wanted to continue relaxing. Jose asked me for a chocolate cookie—probably because he thought I was going to eat them all. I gave him one, possibly the last one. There were a lot of crumbs around and bits of chocolate. I hugged him very tight and said, "Don't ever, ever go away." I think he had on a plain, soft, white shirt.

# Reflections from Family and Friends

After Jose's passing, several friends and family members provided reflections on us as a couple as they observed us. Each shows how much Jose's spirit touched and inspired others. He was truly loved and will be forever missed.

## From Justin Aguinaldo
(our nephew who came to live with me)

### My Uncles
### Uncle Joey and Uncle Ed

I don't even know how I found out that Uncle Ed was not a brother of my dad but a friend of my Uncle Joey. I was young, around six. I remember a big forty- or fifty-year anniversary for Lolo and Lola as being the first time I realized that they were a couple. It actually didn't seem to be that big of a deal to me. I was still young and

I don't think that I had ever thought about homosexuality. It didn't seem abnormal to me, I liked both my uncles and they were really nice. I remember them giving us presents. I still remember the Matchbox car that I got. All the kids lined up and stuck their hand in what seemed like a gargantuan sack full of toys. I wanted a toy car and I got it! I thought that if that is what gay people are like they must be pretty cool. I never heard my family speak badly about them. They didn't talk about them a lot. All I knew for a long time was that they were gay and lived in New York City.

I knew that my Uncle Joey was a pediatrician.

I was surprised when I was invited to go New York with my cousin Joseph. I didn't expect it at all. I didn't know what to expect.

My ideas about homosexuality changed from 1989, when I was six, to the summer of 1997. I grew up in a homophobic rural city. People used "gay" as an adjective for lame, weak, or just bad. Portrayals of gay people in the media made me a bit uncomfortable. I didn't know any other gay people in that town and I didn't see my uncles very much. I didn't feel the same. I was so naive. I soon realized that any concerns were unfounded. Quite the opposite, they were some of the most considerate, generous, and supportive people I've known.

They were very strict with us. They didn't baby us to try and buy our acceptance.

They treated us the way they wanted to be treated, with respect and no special treatment. They were so solid together. I had so much reverence for them. They had such a presence. Joseph and I soon learned to pull our own weight. We volunteered at a day camp in Harlem during the week and hung out in Bellport during the weekend. That was the first time that we worked that hard all week. It was a different type of challenge, not like physical work, even though we marched those kids all over the city in the summer heat. The harder part was fitting in and learning how the kids lived their lives in the inner city. We had to be hard and sensitive at the same time. We would get home and be so tired. I don't think we complained very much. I didn't want to because here I was just starting this grueling schedule and our uncles had been doing it long before us and they not only excelled at what they did but had time to maintain a healthy, meaningful, and loving relationship.

I think that the most surprising thing for me was the quality of their relationship, not that they were gay, successful, or sophisticated New Yorkers. I hadn't experienced anything like it before with the other couples I had been around. It's true I learned to be open-minded about the struggles of ethnic minorities in the low-income communities and I learned about some of the struggles for gay men in American society, but I think my mind opened more to the possibility of a healthy relationship between two human beings. If one is able to understand that before anything else, they cannot help but be in awe of Ed and Joey. They possessed something that I had only seen on TV, an intimate relationship between two people where they focused on each other's strengths and accepted their limitations. They knew when to push each other and when to let it go. It's a balance. It didn't come instantly, they worked for it and they earned and deserved the enjoyment that they created for each other. They were not in-your-face about it. They were fun, a lot of fun.

I left with more optimism for my future. I had been pushed and encouraged, challenged and taught. They changed my entire outlook on my future and I started high school with an advantage on the other kids. That's how I felt when in the past I had always felt like the victim, the person with the disadvantage. I didn't have the money, the clothes, shoes, gadgets, or cars like the other kids, and I always stood out because of that. I also didn't blend into the majority of white people or the minority of Hispanic people. I was always outside of the group in my small town. When I came back I was still an outsider but in a new way. My view of the world was bigger. I didn't feel trapped or doomed to a predictable outcome. I saw what Ed and Joey made for themselves. They worked hard and they pushed past the boundaries of "normal" life. They both grew up with different types of challenges. Joey worked hard as a student of medicine in a developing country to become an amazing doctor and trusted friend to all his many patients, not to mention surviving an accident that took his leg. Ed survived Texas. Haha. I'm halfway joking, but getting to know Ed and going to his home state makes growing up in my town seem like a breeze. I wonder if the people that knew Ed when he was younger could have guessed that he would do such great things for education and the arts. Beyond that they found true love in a partner that greatly complemented each other. Wow, maybe I can do that too.

When my mom woke me up early on the morning of the World Trade Center attacks, I was worried. We were all really worried. I remember the concern in my mom's voice when she opened my door that dim morning. I could tell how much my mom appreciated what my uncles did for me. She knew I had been struggling through adolescence after my dad left. My mom grew up in a somewhat conservative family but she broke from that and has always been very appreciative of my uncles because she could see the change in me when I came back. She could see how her son had grown and matured during his summer on the east coast. She was really worried about my uncles after hearing about the attacks. What a relief to find out that they were OK.

I was in disbelief when I heard that Uncle Joey died. It didn't really sink in until the funeral. I was angry. He was taken. Of all the people to be taken, why Joey? I thought, why couldn't that happen to a person who wasn't helping as many people, or to someone that wasn't as much fun. I was angry. It wasn't until last April that I realized I need to think of it as not having Joey taken away but rather that I was lucky to have him as an uncle and to have had the chance to get to know him and

Uncle Ed. Without them I would still be depressed about being self-suppressed in a small town, thinking that I could never change my situation.

My uncles were the most forceful in getting me to think seriously and follow through with continuing my education. It's a good thing they convinced me when they did because as soon as I got back to school I worked so much harder and learned so much more. This continued even after high school. I didn't think I was actually going to go to college, but there I was. It was hard at times. I would think of Joey. I would think about what it must have been like for Joey in Manila. I would doubt myself. I would compare myself to Joey and all his accomplishments and, at first, I would experience anxiety and fear. I would picture Joey giving me that look. The look where he's thinking, "I know you can do better than that." I would feel like a failure. But then I remembered that Joey was as supportive as he was demanding. He would only push if he knew that it was what should and could be done. For Joey, if it really needed to be done, it could be done. He could ask and achieve such acts of determination and perseverance from his friends and patients because he was living proof of triumph over insurmountable odds. After thinking about Joey more, I would be able overcome my anxiety and continue hacking away at whatever challenge came my way.

# From Fluffy Jones

(my sister)

### Joey

I think of Joey every morning. Yes, every morning.
He and I once had a conversation about washcloths,
in which we both agreed that thick ones were our pet
peeves. You couldn't fit them in your ears for washing.
We preferred the thin ones—so much more useful. So,
every morning during my shower I think of him. It's a
nice way to start the day because it reminds me of other
things I remember about him.

He had the greatest smile and a laugh to go with it.
It warmed up the whole room. In fact, I describe certain
friends as having the "sweet gene," and he surely did have
that. That's not to say he was a wuss; he had a backbone
of steel. He would have to, to do the work he did every
day in the clinics with children from low-income homes
and teenagers with various drug or alcohol problems.
He did it all with fuzzy animals on his stethoscope, a
stand-out bow tie and that smile. Everyone loved him—
children, mothers, and staff. Staff knew that he had an
"illegal" rice cooker and microwave in his office (covered
with a cloth), but no one said a word about it.

He carried on the family tradition of caring for the
next younger sibling by sending his younger brother to
college. But he didn't stop there. He was pretty much
the godfather to all of his siblings and many nieces and
nephews. Several came to New York at one time or

another to stay with him and Buddy, learn about the big city, and sometimes get jobs for the summer. Justin is still there today with the good start and college education that Joey and Buddy provided. Joey looked out for his parents as well.

One time in my life I was grieving the loss of a friend and went to New York to visit for a few days. During that time I was treated royally. I remember that Joey, Buddy, and I went to see *Dream Girls*, such a great show, and that during intermission Joey disappeared for a while. When he returned, he had bought me the cast album. He had such old-fashioned manners that were rare. I was struck by the fact that he made it a point to walk on the outside when we were on the sidewalk and always held out my chair. Wow.

My father loved to get into conversations with him. Daddy loved to talk about world affairs and was pleased to get Joey's opinion about what was going on in the Philippines and other parts of the world. I can just see them with their heads together in serious thought, and then they might just burst out laughing. What a picture.

Joey had style, and he could carry it off when no one else could. How many guys can wear a white suit, bow tie and straw hat the way he could? Classy. He could wear a pink shirt, great sunglasses; you wouldn't see his look in *GQ*. He had his own style, and it worked.

Joey introduced us to a lot of "products." To this day I still use Origins hand cream. I still use the martini glasses and the beautiful oval-shaped red bowl on my kitchen counter. He had such great taste.

He was good with directions—a great navigator.

He liked surprises, such as the wonderful trips he planned for Buddy and the neat extras like a private boat or airplane ride.

He liked the newest, best of everything, like his Porsche.

He was a good cook, including his famous chicken with seven seasonings.

He loved to order dessert, but made everybody else eat most of it.

He liked to sing, sort of an operatic voice, not always on key.

He loved to go to the shore and drive the boat.

He flew to Waco, Texas for our parents' fiftieth wedding anniversary, handed out favors, and patiently answered the guests who frequently asked, "Now, how are you related to the Joneses?"

He loved parties, but rarely drank anything alcoholic. He didn't need to because he was often kinda silly and relaxed anyway.

Everything was not always sunshine and flowers with Joey and Buddy. Not too long after they got together, Joey met someone who swept him off his feet, and he went away for a while. Soon he came back and all was well, but it took me a while to forgive him. You really couldn't stay mad at him for long.

Really, though, I don't know too many gay guys

who had such an eclectic group of friends. Gay people, straight, old people, young, city people, country people, family, neighbors, sophisticates, down-to-earth folks, artsy, square, well-read, and learning to read—they got along with everyone and were accepted by everyone as the long-term couple that they were. Joey and Buddy were proof that a couple of gay guys could be as ordinary as the rest of the world and yet unique and fun.

Fluffy, Kathy, Jose and me at my parents' 50th wedding anniversary, Waco Texas, 1991.

My sister, Fluffy, on the left in New York for her 40th birthday

# From Alec Safreno

(nephew, Chato's son)

**Alec Safreno**
**Spinelli, Period 6**
**September 4, 2006**

"What's wrong, Mom?"

"Alec, Uncle Pet's dead."

Those words changed my life forever. My godfather, and my favorite uncle, was sucked out of my life and into the abyss of death. Suddenly there were no more phone calls, no more visits from him, and no more reason to go to New York. He was gone, just like that and he was only fifty-one years old. When Uncle Pet died, I realized that life's too short and we should enjoy life while it lasts.

Uncle Pet was born on December 13, 1950 in Manila, Philippines. I recall an incident he used to narrate about when he "borrowed" my grandpa's Volkswagen Brasilia. Uncle Pet and Uncle Val (his older brother) crept out of the house just at the crack at dawn and shoved the VW all the way down the narrow alley by the house, to prevent everyone else from hearing the Brasilia's ignition. They embarked on a little joy ride around town and when they got home, grandpa was waiting anxiously to see what kind of punishment he could dish out on them. Now there are two different versions of this story that I've heard: the one my mom tells excludes them from this escapade, while Uncle Pet's places them in the VW enjoying the ride. Uncle

Pet was always trying to get people involved. He was a laid-back comedian, always telling jokes, although most were outdated. I always think he got the funny bone my mom didn't.

In October 2000, Uncle Pet visited the Bay Area. Although he was there only a week, he made the most of his time there by taking my cousin and me to the Tech Museum in San Jose. The Tech Museum was an entertaining experience, especially with Uncle Pet. In each section of the Tech Museum he would accompany us and participate in all the activities and games we played and encouraging us to try new things.

Sometimes it appeared like he was more stoked than I.

When September 11, 2001 came around, it was one the most frightening moments of my life. Uncle Pet lives and works in New York and very close to the Twin Towers. As soon as I heard about the incident, my thoughts turned to him. Is he going to be all right? What happened to him? Those seven hours were the longest in my entire life. There was the anticipation crawling around my head and all I could think about was if he was all right. My mom got hold of him about mid-day and relayed the message later on during the day. Uncle Pet called the next day and told me something incredibly amusing.

"Did you know that the date for September 11 is 911, the emergency phone number?" he said. I have to admit, that was pretty cool. We said our goodbyes over the phone and hung up. Had I known that was the last time I would have talked to him, I would be still on the phone with him today.

March 5, 2002 was an ordinary day. School passed by relatively fast, although boring all the same. When it finally ended, my mom was late as usual, nothing new. I dragged myself over to daycare and awaited her arrival. She got there at about 4:30 p.m. and instead of signing us out, she walked over the far doorway and just slumped against it.

"What's wrong, Mom?" I asked as I approached her.

"Alec, he's dead. Uncle Pet's dead."

Those words hit like a train. I was stunned, confused. He wasn't supposed to die, he was only fifty-one and he just died? I was speechless. The only word I could manage was "*What?*" When I got home I just flung myself into bed and just sat there. I thought about his voice and his face. I recalled all the memories I had, but it only made me think about how those were the only memories I would have. The thought of never seeing him again tore me up inside. I screamed in my head "WHY GOD WHY?" He was only fifty-one years old and died of a cardiovascular problem.

We went to New York on the 13th of March for his funeral and viewing. The viewing was terrible. I loathed it. When I saw the body, to me it just wasn't him. He appeared sad, not happy or joyful like he always was. He was fatter, filled with all kinds of nasty embalming fluids. He was cold, sucked of all blood. Uncle Pet wasn't lying in that coffin, just some corpse.

New York wasn't the same coming back to for the one-year anniversary of his death. Sure, it was New York, with buildings that go higher than the eye can see, or Times Square and all the flashy lights, or even the grid-locked traffic with horns blaring and people screaming. But even with all that going, everything there seem toned down a few notches. We went back to the tomb where his ashes were, talked to him the best way we could, and flew home the same day. The flight home was a life-changing one. Nothing physical happened, but I realized that I shouldn't live sad all my life because there isn't enough time to be sad. I learned that I should value life and do things that I enjoy. If you're going to do something, do it for yourself and enjoy it. Getting back from New York, I recognized that I'm more laid-back and happy with what I'm doing. In the future I may wise up and realize that I can always do what I want, but for now I'm happy where I am in my life. When Uncle Pet died, it hurt and it made me depressed. But when I think about that plane ride home and what I learned from it, the pain and sadness vanished. Joy and happiness rushed back to me, and for a moment, I felt unstoppable.

## From Roy Breimon

(a good friend, an artist, with whom we shared many
good times)

**Dear Ed,**

Once upon a time . . . when I first knew that you were
to be a lifelong friend was when you and Joey and I
were together for that first time. So many firsts—I saw
for the first time a love between men that in later years
would serve to guide me in my relationship with Matt.
I think that it was the ability to see the differences that
you and Joey had, which could have been problematic,
but rather became points of strength and amusement and
life's course.

You know better than anyone who Joey was. I knew
who he was for me—a wild and crazy, caring and loving,
professional and intelligent, funny and patiently serious man. The extremes attracted me, but most of all I
loved to have serious conversations about love, sex, life,
the future, AIDS, money, you, me, Matt, New York,
Round Hill, work, Michael, family, responsibilities, art,
and relationships. I have never been able to have that
same unique rapport with someone else. I miss that. But
I also remember that Joey was ultimately serious, and
I can hear him now saying to me, "OK, but what are
you going to do?" He empowered people. He often gave
encouragement with permission to go ahead and do what
I wanted and do what was best for me, or at least what I
thought would be.

You are suffering more than I know and I hesitate to feel that I can offer any comment other than to support and love you. But I will. You know in your heart that Joey would encourage and empower you to forget the pain, to remember the love you shared, and find happiness. I don't know what will make you happy—Joey was the love of your life, but perhaps around the corner will be another love of your life. I don't mean a man. I don't mean a job or anything specific—just that to be open to the future and to be aware that life is amazing, unpredictable, and full of opportunity that we can never anticipate. I want the best for you now and for the rest of your life.

Love,
Roy

**Roy at my 40th birthday party**

# From Sarah Levine

(a lifelong friend of mine from Texas)

### Lovely Encounters; Lofty Inspirations

The very first time I met Jose (Joey to me), I could tell what a special man he was and that he and Ed (whom I have always called Buddy) had an exceptional relationship. Living in Texas, I didn't have the occasion to be with them nearly often enough; but when I did, I stayed at their house for several days at a time, so I had the opportunity to witness that extraordinary relationship up-close and in their own surroundings. It was clear that they loved each other with a love that is extremely rare and beautiful. Of all my friends, straight and gay, they had by far the most committed and caring relationship. In fact, we often laugh about it and comment that their bond lasted while those of our heterosexual friends did not—my own included. It was a joy to be with them, although I have to admit that there were moments of jealousy that they had that glorious relationship my life lacked at the time.

My memories of the two of them together are many and grand. I remember once when I was visiting them in New York, we went out for a lovely dinner in midtown. After a sumptuous meal, Joey, who knew how much I loved sweets, announced that he was going to take us out for dessert; so we piled into the car and drove up to Café Lalo. Buddy just rolled his eyes and, although I am sure he didn't think that addition to the evening was necessary, didn't say a word, and just went along for a good time.

That's just the way their relationship was. Neither of them would ever embarrass the other by not supporting a decision. It was in these little ways that they showed respect for one another. Their thoughtfulness of each other showed up in ways most people never think of or are too self-centered to give freely. I witnessed that time and again with Buddy and Joey.

I think my most wonderful memory of being with Buddy and Joey took place one summer when they invited me to join them at their house in the Catskills. Buddy and I arrived earlier as Joey had to work. We spent a gorgeous day pulling climbing roses off of the house and puttering around the grounds. We picked apples from the trees on the property and made a delicious apple pie together. We shopped at the farmers market and prepared wonderful fresh meals. On the night that Joey came up to join us, we had a fabulous supper and way too much wine by candlelight in the little house that sat right on the river's edge with the sound of the water rushing by as our music. A loose arrangement of flowers from their garden decorated our rustic table. It was an amazing evening that I shall remember for as long as I live—so relaxing, so beautiful, and wonderful to be with such dear friends. Their comfortable way with each other created an atmosphere of total serenity. The rest of the long weekend was equally wonderful and relaxing. It was one of the most refreshing vacations I have ever had. I shall treasure that memory forever!

I happened to be in New York one time when the Miss America Pageant took place. Joey turned the television on and started to watch the pageant. I started talking over the sound of the television, and Buddy quickly informed me, in his kind and gentle way, that we could not talk while Joey was watching a beauty pageant. His sensitivity to Joey and the way he protected and cared for him touched my heart deeply. They had such respect and regard for each other's needs and hurried to make sure those needs were met. I loved watching that genuine esteem they shared and how obvious their mutual admiration was. It went far beyond just love for one another. They cherished each other beyond love.

There are a million wonderful memories: rooftop garden parties, the New York Botanical Garden at Christmas, cooking spaghetti, eating by candlelight (Joey loved candles!). One very special memory was meeting Joey's warm and gracious family and singing and laughing with all of them in their very crowded apartment. I loved listening to Joey tell us about his "peeds," welcoming in the new year New York-style and just sitting and enjoying a glass of wine together. Each is its own treasure to me, but what I remember with the most admiration is simply the way the two of them interacted. There was such tenderness and reverence between them. It was striking to me how they nurtured each other. Even though they were very different in so many ways, they were the perfect complement for each other; yin and yang. Time did not make them more alike as you sometimes see in a relationship. Each kept his own identity, valuing their differences while honoring their union. There was always more give than take. Respect was at the root of every encounter, even disagreements. Theirs was a pure love without condition, without judgment. They did not speak in unison; they spoke in harmony. That is what gave their partnership the magic.

Touch is a central element of my relationship with my husband. We hold hands, I put my hand on his shoulder, he puts his hand on the small of my back as we walk into a room and we sneak little kisses when no one is looking. That is the way we express our love. I never saw Buddy and Joey do this. In fact, the only time I ever saw them kiss was at midnight on New Year's Eve once. But there was no question about the passion they had for each other. It was expressed with a glance, a gesture— not physically (at least not in front of me). I don't know if that came from the fact that they were a gay couple and felt that they should not show physical affection publicly or if it was just their way. But there was a quietly powerful connection between them that did not require touch. Each knew beyond doubt that they were loved.

I have known and loved Buddy for fifty years, I guess; but it was those fantastic twenty-one years when he and Joey were together that he had that beautiful inner glow. It was contagious—I always felt happy and at peace when I was with them. Their positive chemistry touched me deeply and has definitely served as a shining example for me in my relationship with my husband. I am forever grateful for that.

What made Buddy and Joey's relationship special? It was so many things, small and large. I wish I could capture it in words, but it was something not-of-this-world. I have to say that I have never known another like it. Try as I have to emulate it in my own relationship, as much as I love and adore my husband, I have fallen short of treating him with the grace and gentleness Joey and Buddy showed each other. Their bond was one-of-a-kind. My heart is filled with joy and thanksgiving for the gift of knowing Buddy and Joey together!

Jose with my lifelong friend, Sarah, and her daughter, Jennie, at my parents' 50th wedding anniversary, Waco, Texas, 1991.

# From Tante Aguinaldo
(Jose's youngest brother)

### *My Short Memoir of Jose (Pet) Aguinaldo and Edward Jones*
### By Tante Aguinaldo

During my college years, Jose, my big brother, and Ed, have always encouraged me to come and visit them in New York. Their openness echoes to me very clearly that they wanted to share their special lives as an interracial gay couple. I knew how truly important this was to both of them. Up until this day, this holds genuinely true because Ed always welcomes anyone in Jose's family to visit.

I met them for the first time as a couple in winter of 1983. I learned about their relationship through Jose whenever I got the chance to speak to them over the phone. My first impression was how formal their relationship was. I could feel the great respect and formality within them. Although not intentional, I felt tremendous pressure or widely intimidated on how to behave in front of them. My experience with an interracial and gay couple was zero, and my instinct did not lead me on how I should address certain situation in a correct manner. I decided to just let things happen and go with a flow, and try my best to get to know them as a couple in their environment.

When I arrived in New York that year, I saw them at the La Guardia airport. Their first words were "Welcome to New York," and they said this very graciously and with warmth. I always have the vivid recollection of Jose's gesture of handing me the coat that I will need to wear. After all, it was good thirty degrees outside that night. Jose and Ed hugged me, and I felt very welcome indeed. The trip to their apartment on East 66th Street was captivating. Seeing Manhattan's skyscrapers on the ground level for the first time was very impressive, the glittering city lights were hypnotic, and you could sense the history of New York as the biggest financial institution and endless art culture in the entire world. I was very happy that I would be learning great new things about them in their own special world, and not bad to explore the great city either.

I was very thankful that I made this first trip because this was the beginning of a great relationship with my dearest brother Jose and Ed. During our many lounging conversations and philosophical exchanges, I am very fond of calling my brother with his nickname, which is Pet. My instincts tell me that Filipinos have this endearing quality about confusing other cultures, specifically the white culture, because of different nicknames. We laugh about it, and sometimes, they become an inside joke between Jose and Ed. It never seemed to amaze me how genuinely loving they were in front of their friends and me.

My brother Pet was the explorer, and I always call him "the guy with the itchy feet." Because of his educational background, learning is always important. This

holds true for Ed because both of them are practicing professionals in their respected fields, and they were
highly educated couple. So, because of their background,
I understood the formality within their relationship.
They addressed themselves very proper, they wore their
suits with great dignity, and they have an uncanny taste
of how they expressed their fashion. They dressed themselves very well. I accepted their way of life because their
wonderful personalities just simply matched. They were
incredible, and I tried to emulate their approach in life.

I never had the chance to ask Pet how they met.
Luckily, Ed was able to fill in the blanks after long years
when I finally had the courage to ask. Their relationship
started when they decided to meet in the bar way back
in 1981. This was the defining moment for both of them.
According to Ed, Pet was the first one who expressed
eloquently to plunge into the relationship, and this was a
great mutual respect and love between Pet and Ed. They
continued their great relationship throughout the years.

As the years passed, I continued to visit them in
New York. They eventually moved to the West Side of
Manhattan, and they bought a beautiful country place
in Long Island as well. These places were my two favorite places to visit because these places were very special to
me in reference to the happy, sad, and somber moments
for both of them, and to me. When their careers were
flourishing, they grew more and more as a solid couple
because life was simply good. Pet's distant family was
also growing, and his nieces and nephews were increasing

and becoming teenagers. Pet and Ed shifted their focus to encourage these little munchkins to visit them during holidays, and summers at the Long Island country house. They provided these great moments to them. Specifically, Christina, Justin, Connor, Aidan, Alana, and other children from the west coast that have commonly shared great moments and stories with them.

The couple wanted their nieces and nephews to be part of their lives, and with the hope to see them as a great role model regardless of their sexual orientation. Of course, there are issues, and not all members of the family were very open about their special relationship. Because Filipino culture is not very articulate to talk about gay couples, but they simply accept them as part of the family. However, this does not help the dysfunctional relationship when people start to behave conservatively behind closed doors. Our stories of Pet and Ed lend itself to critical eyes of our own generation of children to come. Perhaps, their wonderful story gives way to the openness they offered me during the time when I first met them in the cold winter night of 1983.

Of course, life was not complete if you do not experience sadness. During the mid-'80s, Pet and Ed grew apart in their relationship to a point where they almost broke up. At the time, my relationship with them became more of a how are you and how is life over the phone. I was preoccupied with my life and work. I seldom visited them in New York. It was more of growing apart with everyone being busy with his or her lives.

When Pet wanted more out of his relationship, he never confided with me during the trouble years, and neither did Ed. I respected them, and it was not a comfortable situation. The only logical explanation was to go back to the formality of my relationship with them and their relationship with me when open communication was the norm. We all became distant, and I could no longer talk to him as my big brother Pet. I was not comfortable prying with his life with Ed, let alone that I am just their little brother. In other words, their openness was being shuttered. At the time, I was also busy taking care of my family, and not attending the garden, to continue my loving and caring relationship with my two favorite people in the world, and that relationship was disappearing in front of my eyes.

When Pet visited us in the Bay Area in 1997, to my surprise, he shared one of his challenges in life, which was to adopt a child. This conversation was not an open discussion with Ed according to Pet. However, when it was open for discussion, the moment was lost, and Pet can no longer support the idea. His biggest fear was he thought that he would be the only one to take care of the child. He was afraid that it would be too much work and effort to sacrifice their own lifestyle. That conversation struck a nerve to me because I know that it takes a lot of human sacrifice to nurture a child in this world, and I completely understood where he was coming from. I was truly encouraged that Pet and Ed were sincere and brave for giving a thought to take care of a child in this world.

Their years went by without realizing their dream of having their adopted child in their lives. However, other things were in their minds on how they can fulfill and dedicate their lives to parenthood. They have not relinquished their dream that someday they will be parents.

In 1999, Pet and Ed became an uncle again with my firstborn child, Tino Julian Aguinaldo. I always thought that this was a very special moment for Pet, Ed, and me. To celebrate the occasion, we flew to New York to have a second christening for Tino with Pet and Ed as the godfathers for Tino. The occasion was special indeed. Their gay couple neighbor, Carl and John, were there. Reggie and her two children were also with us to enjoy the festivity. Pictures were taken to capture the memory with Uncle Pet and Uncle Ed. Although Tino was several months old, I wanted him to cherish the moment later on his life that Uncle Pet and Uncle Ed were two special people in my life, and we celebrated his christening in their Long Island house. I knew by heart that Pet and Ed were really touched by our gesture because this was the only celebration that took place in their own world. They have always sacrificed their time and energy to visit and celebrate some occasion in the Bay Area.

I honestly believed that Tino's christening rekindled their passion to become parents again, and this time in a different way. Justin Aguinaldo and Joseph Torneros visited them one summer, and Justin fell in love with New York right away. He genuinely expressed his interest to join Pet and Ed to go to college in New York. At the time, Pet and Ed were thinking about moving out of the West Side penthouse into a new place much bigger so that they can accommodate Justin. I never imagined Pet and Ed so happy about the idea, and even for a short time, they would experience some parenthood for the first time in their lives. I was very happy for them as well as for Justin. It never occurred to me that sometimes life gives way to the deserving couple that were yearning some balance to their lives, and Justin was the person that will give that balance to them. For Jose, my dearest brother Pet, this was short-lived.

In September of 2001, my second child was born. I consulted Jose and Ed that I will be naming our child Francis Jose, and I could sense that Jose was crying over the phone during our brief conversation. I knew that naming the child after him will be special, and he was honored. He cried with happiness. I've never seen him act that way. He did not have the chance to get to know Francis Jose, but Ed was able to find a way to bridge that relationship between Francis, Jose, and Ed.

His untimely death in 2002 was one of the most painful experiences in my life, and to everyone else who were touched by Jose's enigmatic, forgiving, and courageous personality. I came to realize that the openness of Jose and Ed throughout the years was their child after all. She was born in winter of 1983 during my first visit with them. They took care of her throughout their tough times of their wonderful years together. Now, Ed is the sole father of this openness, and I could

see the resemblance of Jose and Ed that is being shared
to all of us, and to the next generation of their nieces
and nephews.

Jose and family at his youngest brother's graduation. In the
family tradition, Jose supported his brother's education.

Yours truly with Godson Tino in Bellport. He was chris-
tened there.

# From Reggie Schmitt

(Jose's cousin)

## Attracting Opposites

The doctor came from the far east, and through the
Golden Gate.

From the center of Texas, he looked up and
headed north.

At the stroke of midnight, they didn't kiss
But their New Year of 1981 began in New York City.
Buying bow ties on the Upper eastside,
Potted hibiscus on the penthouse of West 100th
Babes squeal at the sight of the white coat at
Gouverneur

Wall Street man in a suit, sharing the wealth of JP,
Measles, mumps and rubella
Monet, Keith Haring and Carmen
Art & medicine,
At the end of the day, cures everything.
What about Mitali East for dinner?
The Village, Loisaida or Jackson Heights? No, *not*
New Jersey!

Painting the barn red in the Catskills,
Antiquing in Eastport on the way to Bellport bay
Speed boat & faster Boxter.
Water ski on One ski. Hop on One foot.
Why? *Why not??*
Open-mindedness. Focused.
Nonchalant, compassionate, pained, perseverant.

Fun and frenzied. Both or solo.
Spontaneous integration,
Contrasting types,
Loving always.
Ed and Joey.

# From Susan Loonsk
(former roommate)

It's been a long time since we all lived on West 21st Street. I remember the fun times with Jose. We would sit on the living room couch just laughing. I couldn't even tell you what we were laughing about, but we did laugh a lot!

I also remember Jose cooking Adobo. He would warn me it doesn't smell very good but it did indeed taste very good!

Jose would see me off on what he called my "Weekend Getaways" as I left to see a boyfriend in Brooklyn.

Jose was a good man. A very caring man.

**Jose and Susan at 210 West 21st Street, 1981/82**

# Dear Mom

(Letter to Jose's Mom around 2003)

**Dear Mom,**

This is a message from Ed.

I love to tell my friends a story about how you welcomed me into the family many years ago. It was 1981. I was concerned about what you and Dad might think of me—this Texas/New Yorker who lived with Jose. But you made me feel at home and at ease right away.

I have this great memory of my first trip to visit the family. You told me and Jose, "This is where you can stay." And you tossed two pillows into a bedroom where we would stay for a few days. You didn't worry over the details. I enjoy describing this moment to friends of ours to illustrate how you and Dad were so accepting of me at a time when many people were not so accepting of couples like us.

Over the years (twenty-one years), you never hesitated to make me feel at home. And over time, you made me feel part of the family. I can't tell you how much it means to me that you have been so supportive since Jose passed away. While all of the brothers and sisters have been magnificent in their loving response to me, it is you who have set the standard for everyone else. It is your strength and loving acceptance that sets an example for my generation and the next, and the next.

Many times, when I describe Jose to friends, I say

that his strength and determination came from you. That is very clear to me. Meanwhile, Dad's sense of history and comradeship also were strong characteristics that showed up in Jose's personality. Those traits were very similar to my own father, and I deeply regret that those two wonderful men never met. I am very happy that you—and most of the family—have come to know my mother. She has taken so much joy from her memories of you and the family.

Please accept my gratitude for making me feel a genuine part of the family over all these years. Without you, it just wouldn't be. I am deeply grateful to you.

I admire you, I love you, and I'll never forget you.

Ed

# Afterword

It was an early winter morning in our farmhouse in Catskill. We were standing next to our bedroom window in our night clothes watching the snow fall on our property sloping down to the creek. Jose was leaning against me without his leg.

"Oh Ed, are we always going to be like this?"

"Yes, Jose," I said.

# Acknowledgments

I wish to thank all family and friends without whom I would not have survived Jose's passing in any remotely normal condition. Especially, I thank my sister, Fluffy Jones, and the entire Aguinaldo family, in particular Christina Valenzuela, Justin Aguinaldo, and Rosario (Chato) Safreno. In addition, I greatly appreciate all of those who contributed "Reflections" here. They added a dimension to this memoir that I could not convey. I am grateful to my friend Anne Focke, who offered valuable guidance to me as I struggled through the early drafts of this book. I also thank my editor, Patrick Price, who put thoughtful, professional touches on the completed manuscript. Finally, I express my gratitude to my husband, Jeffrey Twu, who was respectful of the memory of Jose from day one and who continues to be a loving and supportive partner in all happy and sad times.

# About the Author

Ed Jones was born and raised in Waco, Texas. Toward the end of his graduate studies, he moved to New York City where he established the education department at The New Museum of Contemporary Art. Subsequently, he transitioned to a career in philanthropy, primarily focusing on funding the arts and higher education. After his retirement, Ed has been teaching English at the New York Public Library to students from around the world. They have added immeasurably to his own education. Ed lives in New York City with his wonderful husband, Jeffrey Twu. He would welcome reader comments. He can be reached at: casiveinte45@yahoo.com

Artist's painting by Deborah Boelter